The Original
Summer Bridge Activities™

First to Second Grade

W9-BFS-502

SBA was created by
Michele D. Van Leeuwen

written by
Julia Ann Hobbs
Carla Dawn Fisher

illustrations by
Magen Mitchell
Amanda Sorensen

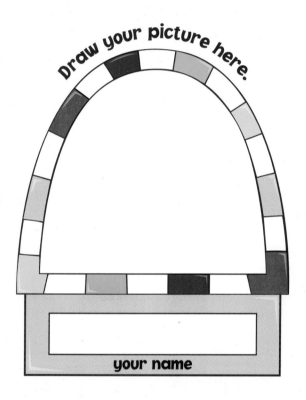

Draw your picture here.

your name

Summer Learning Staff
Clareen Arnold, Lori Davis, Melody Feist, Aimee Hansen, Christopher Kugler,
Kristina Kugler, Molly McMahon, Paul Rawlins, Liza Richards, Linda Swain

Design
Andy Carlson, Robyn Funk

Cover Art
Karen Maizel

ISBN: 1-59441-727-X

Super Summer Science pages © 2002 The Wild Goose Company and Carson-Dellosa.

20 19 18 17 16 15 14 13 12 11

Dear Parents,

The summer months are a perfect time to reconnect with your child on many levels after a long school year. Your personal involvement is so important to your child's immediate and long-term academic success. No matter how wonderful your child's classroom experience is, your involvement outside the classroom will make it that much better!

Summer Bridge Activities™ is the original summer workbook developed to help parents support their children academically while away from school, and we strive to improve the content, the activities, and the resources to give you the highest quality summer learning materials available. Ten years ago, we introduced **Summer Bridge Activities**™ to a small group of teachers and parents after I had successfully used it to help my first grader prepare for the new school year. It was a hit then, and it continues to be a hit now! Many other summer workbooks have been introduced since, but **Summer Bridge Activities**™ continues to be the one that both teachers and parents ask for most. We take our responsibility as the leader in summer education seriously and are always looking for new ways to make summer learning more fun, more motivating, and more effective to help make your child's transition to the new school year enjoyable and successful!

We are now excited to offer you even more bonus summer learning materials online at www.SummerBridgeActivities.com! This site has great resources for both parents and kids to use on their own and together. An expanded summer reading program where kids can post their own book reviews, writing and reading contests with great prizes, assessment tests, travel packs, and even games are just a few of the additional resources that you and your child will have access to with the included **Summer Bridge Activities**™ Online Pass Code.

Summer Learning has come a long way over the last 10 years, and we are glad that you have chosen to use **Summer Bridge Activities**™ to help your children continue to discover the world around them by using the classroom skills they worked so hard to obtain!

Have a wonderful summer!

Michele Van Leeuwen and the Summer Learning Staff!

Hey Kids!

We bet you had a great school year!
Congratulations on all your hard work! We just want to say
that we're proud of the great things you did this year, and we're excited
to have you spend time with us over the summer. Have fun with your
Summer Bridge Activities™ workbook, and visit us online at
www.**SummerBridgeActivities**.com for more fun, cool, and exciting stuff!

Have a great summer!

The T. O. C. (Table of Contents)

Official Pass Code

| al0604r |

Log on to www.SummerBridgeActivities.com and join!

Sections of SBA

 There are three sections in SBA: the first and second review, the third previews.

 Each section begins with an SBA Motivational Calendar.

 Each day your child will complete an activity in reading, writing, math, and language. The activities become progressively more challenging.

 Each page is numbered by day.

Here's what you will find inside

Summer Bridge Activities™

Exercises in **Summer Bridge Activities™** (SBA) are easy to understand and presented in fun and creative ways that motivate children to review familiar skills while being progressively challenged. In addition to basic skills in reading, writing, math, and language arts, SBA contains activities that challenge and reinforce reading comprehension, phonemic awareness, and letter, word, and number recognition for young learners.

Daily exercises review and preview skills in reading, writing, math, and language arts. Activities are presented in half-page increments so kids do not get overwhelmed and are divided into three sections to correlate with traditional summer vacation.

Bonus Super Summer Science pages provide hands-on science activities.

A Summer Reading List introduces kids to some of today's popular titles as well as the classics. Kids can rate books they read and log on to www.**SummerBridgeActivities**.com to post reviews, find more great titles, and participate in national reading and writing contests!

Motivational Calendars begin each section and help kids achieve all summer long.

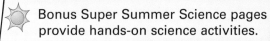

Discover Something New lists offer fun and creative activities that teach kids with their hands and get them active and learning.

Grade-specific flashcards provide a great way to reinforce basic skills in addition to the written exercises.

Removable Answer Pages ensure that parents know as much as their kids!

A Certificate of Completion for parents to sign congratulates kids for their work and welcomes them to the grade ahead.

A grade-appropriate, official Summer Fun pass code gives kids and parents online access to more bonus games, contests, and resources at www.**SummerBridgeActivities**.com.

Here are some groups who say our books are great!

Mr. Fredrickson

10 Ways to Maximize
The Original Summer Bridge Activities™

 First, let your child explore the book. Flip through the pages and look at the activities with your child to help him become familiar with the book.

 Help select a good time for reading or working on the activities. Suggest a time before your child has played outside and becomes too tired to do the work.

 Provide any necessary materials. A pencil, ruler, eraser, crayons, or reference works may be required.

 Offer positive guidance. Remember, the activities are not meant to be tests. You want to create a relaxed and positive attitude toward learning. Work through at least one example on each page with your child. "Think aloud" and show your child how to solve problems.

 Give your child plenty of time to think. You may be surprised by how much children can do on their own.

 Stretch your child's thinking beyond the page. If you are reading a book, you might ask, "What do you think will happen next?" or "What would you do if this happened to you?" Encourage your child to talk about her interests and observations about the world around her.

 Reread stories and occasionally flip through completed pages. Completed pages and books will be a source of pride to your child and will help show how much he accomplished over the summer.

 Read and work on activities while outside. Take the workbook out in the backyard or on a family campout. It can be fun wherever you are!

 Encourage siblings, relatives, and neighborhood friends to help with reading and activities. Other children are often perfect for providing the one-on-one attention necessary to reinforce reading skills.

 Give plenty of approval! Stickers and stamps are effective for recognizing a job well done. At the end of the summer, your child can feel proud of her accomplishments and will be eager for school to start.

Skills List

Language Arts/Reading

- [ ] Recognizes uppercase letters
- [ ] Recognizes lowercase letters
- [ ] Can print uppercase letters correctly
- [ ] Can print lowercase letters correctly
- [ ] Knows alphabetical sequence
- [ ] Recognizes beginning consonant sounds
- [ ] Recognizes final consonant sounds
- [ ] Recognizes short vowel sounds
- [ ] Recognizes long vowel sounds
- [ ] Knows L blends: bl, cl, fl, gl, pl, sl
- [ ] Knows beginning blends: sk, sm, sn, sp, st, sw, tw
- [ ] Knows R blends: br, cr, dr, fr, gr, pr, tr
- [ ] Knows digraphs: ch, sh, th, ng
- [ ] Recognizes r-controlled vowels: ar, er, ir, or, ur
- [ ] Can sound out simple words
- [ ] Can identify characters in a story
- [ ] Can identify the main idea of a story
- [ ] Can identify the setting of a story
- [ ] Can identify the conclusion of a story
- [ ] Uses letter sounds to write words
- [ ] Draws illustrations to match sentences
- [ ] Can identify compound words
- [ ] Can identify nouns
- [ ] Can identify pronouns
- [ ] Can identify verbs
- [ ] Can identify linking verbs: am, is, are, was, were
- [ ] Knows how to form plurals with s and es
- [ ] Uses punctuation correctly: period, question mark, exclamation point
- [ ] Knows how to form basic contractions
- [ ] Uses capitalization correctly
- [ ] Recognizes rhyming words
- [ ] Recognizes antonyms, synonyms, and homonyms
- [ ] Is beginning to read and write for pleasure

Parent:

Exercises for these skills can be found inside **Summer Bridge Activities™** and can be used for extra practice. The skills lists are a great way to discover your child's strengths or what skills may need additional reinforcement.

Skills List

Math

- [ ] Counts and recognizes numbers to 100
- [ ] Counts by 2s to 100
- [ ] Counts by 5s to 100
- [ ] Counts by 10s to 100
- [ ] Completes simple patterns
- [ ] Sorts by one or two attributes
- [ ] Can sequence events
- [ ] Can name eight basic shapes
- [ ] Knows addition facts to 10
- [ ] Knows subtraction facts to 10
- [ ] Can write number sentences using +, −, and =
- [ ] Knows addition facts to 18
- [ ] Knows subtraction facts to 18
- [ ] Can read and create a graph
- [ ] Knows ordinal numbers (first–tenth)
- [ ] Reads number words
- [ ] Understands place value to the ones place
- [ ] Understands place value to the tens place
- [ ] Understands place value to the hundreds place
- [ ] Adds two-digit numbers, no regrouping
- [ ] Subtracts two-digit numbers, no regrouping
- [ ] Performs column addition with three single-digit numbers
- [ ] Recognizes money: penny, nickel, dime, quarter, half-dollar
- [ ] Knows the value of money: penny, nickel, dime, quarter, half-dollar
- [ ] Can count money using pennies, nickels, and dimes
- [ ] Can tell time on the hour
- [ ] Can tell time on the half hour
- [ ] Can measure using inches
- [ ] Can identify fractions: 1/2, 1/3, 1/4
- [ ] Uses problem-solving strategies to complete math problems

Summertime = Reading Time!

We all know how important reading is, but this summer show kids how GREAT the adventures of reading really are! Summer learning and summer reading go hand-in-hand, so here are a few ideas to get you up and going:

Encourage your child to read out loud to you and make a theatrical performance out of even the smallest and simplest read. Have fun with reading and impress the family at the campsite next to you at the same time!

Establish a time to read together each day. Make sure and ask each other about what you are reading and try to relate it to something that may be going on within the family.

Show off! Let your child see you reading for enjoyment and talk about the great things that you are discovering from what you read. Laugh out loud, stamp your feet—it's summertime!

Sit down with your child and establish a summer reading program. Use our cool Summer Reading List and Summer Reading Program at www.**SummerBridgeActivities**.com, or visit your local bookstore and, of course, your local library. Encourage your child to select books on topics he is interested in and on his reading level. A rule of thumb for selecting books at the appropriate reading level is to choose a page and have your child read it out loud. If he doesn't know five or more of the words on the page, the book may be too difficult.

Use your surroundings (wherever you are) to show your child how important reading is on a daily basis. Read newspaper articles, magazines, stories, and road maps during the family vacation...just don't get lost!

Find books that tie into your child's experiences. If you are going fishing or boating, find a book on the subject to share. This will help your child learn and develop interests in new things.

Get library cards! Set a regular time to visit the library and encourage your child to have her books read and ready to return so she is ready for the next adventure! Let your child choose her own books. It will encourage her to read and pursue her own interests.

Make up your own stories! This is great fun and can be done almost anywhere—in the car, on camping trips, in a canoe, on a plane! Encourage your child to tell the story with a beginning, middle, AND end. To really challenge each other, start with the end, then middle, and then the beginning—yikes!

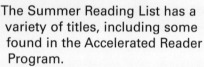

Books to Read

The Summer Reading List has a variety of titles, including some found in the Accelerated Reader Program.

We recommend parents read to pre-kindergarten through 1st grade children 5–10 minutes each day and then ask questions about the story to reinforce comprehension. For higher grade levels, we suggest the following daily reading times: grades 1–2, 10–20 min.; grades 2–3, 20–30 min.; grades 3–4, 30–45 min.; grades 4–6, 45–60 min.

It is important to decide an amount of reading time and write it on the SBA Motivational Calendar.

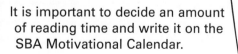

Summer Reading List

Fill in the stars and rate your favorite (and not so favorite) books here and online at
www.SummerBridgeActivities.com!

1 = I struggled to finish this book.
2 = I thought this book was pretty good.
3 = I thought this book rocked!
4 = I want to read this book again and again!

Why Mosquitoes Buzz in People's Ears: A West African Tale

Aarderna, Verna

America's Champion Swimmer: Gertrude Ederle

Adler, David A.

Do you know who the first woman to swim the English Channel was? And did you know she swam faster than the men?

Miss Nelson Is Missing!

Allard, Harry

When Miss Nelson goes missing and is replaced with a scary substitute, the kids in Room 207 learn lessons about good behavior and kindness.

The Grey Lady and the Strawberry Snatcher

Bang, Molly

And I Mean It, Stanley

Bonsall, Crosby

Molly's Pilgrim

Cohen, Barbara

Are You My Mother?

Eastman, P. D.

Corduroy

Freeman, Don

My Ballet Class

Isadora, Rachel

I Want to Be a Clown

Johnson, Sharon

The Eye Book

LeSieg, Theo

Frog and Toad series

Lobel, Arnold

Caps for Sale

Slobodkina, Esphyr

Put Me in the Zoo

Lopshire, Robert

Ira Sleeps Over

Waber, Bernard

 Ira wants to sleep over at Reggie's house. But can he really leave his teddy bear at home?

Make Way for Ducklings

McCloskey, Robert

Little Bear

Minarik, Else Holmelund

The Biggest Bear

Ward, Lynd

 What is Johnny Orchard supposed to do when his little bear cub grows up to be a big "bear" of a problem?

The Nose Book

Perkins, Al

In a Dark, Dark Room

Schwartz, Alvin

Math Curse

Scieszka, Jon

Mike and the Bike

Ward, Michael

 Mike takes off on an adventure around the world with his best friend—his bike.

That's Silly

Sleator, William

Join the SBA Kids Summer Reading Club!

Quick! Get Mom or Dad to help you log on and join the SBA Kids Summer Reading Club. You can find more great books, tell your friends about your favorite titles, and even win cool prizes! Log on to www.SummerBridgeActivities.com and sign up today.

Complete the counting patterns.

10	20		40			70			100

5	10	15			35	40		
55		70			90			

2	4		8		12			18		22
	26			32					42	

Write the short and long vowels.

EXAMPLE:

c_a_ke

t____ba

b____x

d____ck

t____re

l____mp

m____lk

t____e

"Where is it?" Write down whether the object is in front of, next to, or behind the other object.

1. The slide is

_____

_____ the boy.

2. The swing set is _____ the slide.

3. The sand pit is _____ the swing set.

Catch each butterfly. Put each one in the right net by drawing a line to where it belongs.

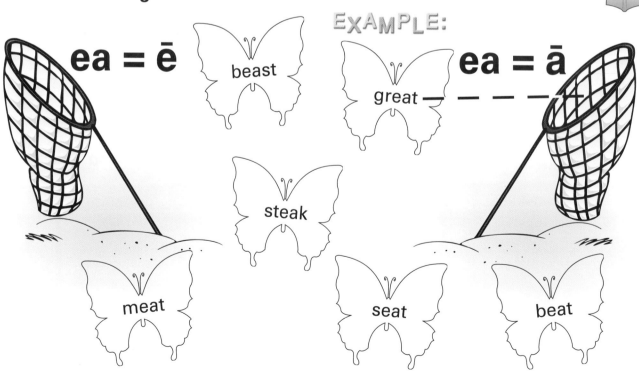

ea = ē

beast

EXAMPLE:

great — — — —

ea = ā

steak

meat

seat

beat

Decide how many tens and how many ones make up each number.

EXAMPLE:

26 = __2__ tens __6__ ones   41 = _____ ones _____ tens

45 = _____ tens _____ ones   84 = _____ tens _____ ones

65 = _____ ones _____ tens   72 = _____ ones _____ tens

17 = _____ ones _____ tens   39 = _____ tens _____ ones

50 = _____ tens _____ ones   51 = _____ ones _____ tens

97 = _____ ones _____ tens   100 = _____ tens _____ ones

Read the sentence; then follow the directions.

Denise hugged her dog three times.

1. Circle the word hugged.
2. Draw a box around the word that tells who Denise hugged.
3. Underline the word that tells who hugged the dog.
4. Draw a picture of Denise and her dog.

Number these sentences in the order they happened.

FACTOID
Talk about a fish out of water! The lung fish can survive out of the water for almost four years.

☐ The sun came out. It was a pretty day.

☐ The thunder roared, and the lightning flashed.

☐ It rained and rained.

☐ Sue put her umbrella away.

☐ Sue walked under her umbrella.

☐ The clouds came, and the sky was dark.

Finish the story.

Once there was a sun. The happy sun loved to shine its bright rays onto the earth because...

_____

_____

_____

_____

_____

_____

_____

_____

Draw the hands to match the time, or write the time to match the hands.

2:30

___ : ___

10:30

___ : ___

5:00

___ : ___

Circle the letters that spell the beginning sound of each picture.

EXAMPLE:

(ch) wh sh th

ch wh sh th

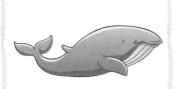
ch wh sh th

ch wh sh th

ch wh sh th

ch wh sh th

ch wh sh th

ch wh sh th

Read and decide.

FACTOID
Ever wondered how night butterflies avoid hungry bats? They have ears on their wings!

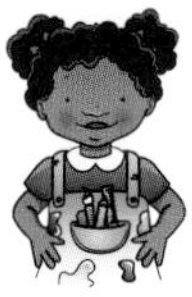

One day, a man went on a hunt. He hunted for a long time. At the end of the day, he was very happy. What do you think the man found? Did he find something to eat? Did he find something pretty? Did he find something funny? Decide what the man found and draw a picture of it!

Put the following words in alphabetical order.

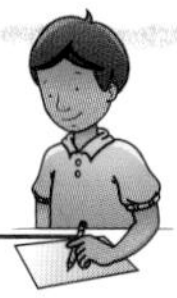

he
up
fat
little
big
stop
and
out
slow
go

1. ____________________
2. ____________________
3. ____________________
4. ____________________
5. ____________________
6. ____________________
7. ____________________
8. ____________________
9. ____________________
10. ____________________

Solve these problems.

1. Rob found five bees. Denise found five bees. How many bees are there in all?

_____ bees

$$\begin{array}{r} \square \\ +\ \square \\ \hline \square \end{array}$$

2. Matt has seven fish. Matt bought five more fish. How many fish are there in all?

_____ fish

$$\begin{array}{r} \square \\ +\ \square \\ \hline \square \end{array}$$

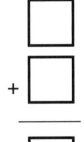

Draw and color the correct number of gum balls in each machine.

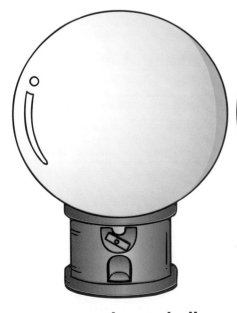

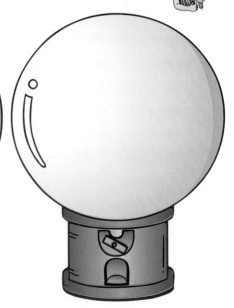

seven red gum balls   **ten orange gum balls**   **five blue gum balls**

Read each story. Choose the best title.

A rabbit can jump. Frogs can jump too—but a kangaroo is the best jumper of all!
1. Jumping Rabbits
2. Animals That Jump
3. Hop! Hop! Hop!

Tanner is up now. He hits the ball. "Run, Tanner, run! Run to first base, then to second. Can you run to home base?"

1. Running 2. Tanner Plays
3. Tanner's Baseball Game

Allie put on her blue coat and her fuzzy, pink hat. Then she put on her warm, white mittens.

1. A Hot Day
2. Getting Ready to Go
3. Allie Likes to Play

Rob gave his pet dog a bone. He gave his fat cat some canned cat food. He also fed the ducks.
1. Feeding the Animals
2. Rob's Animals
3. Cats, Dogs, and Birds

Make these words plural, meaning more than one, by adding -s or -es.

EXAMPLE:

1. cat ___**cats**___

2. kitten _____

3. glass _____

4. inch _____

5. truck _____

6. dish _____

7. fan _____

8. clock _____

9. wish _____

10. brush _____

11. ball _____

12. dog _____

Subtract and fill in the answers on the outer circle.

EXAMPLE:

Circle and write the word that goes with each picture.

glove   _____

- - - - - - - - - - - - - - - - - - - -

glue   _____

flower   _____

- - - - - - - - - - - - - - - - - - - -

flag   _____

flashlight   _____

- - - - - - - - - - - - - - - - - - - -

fly   _____

Use the following words to fill in the blanks:

Who	What	Where	Why	When

1. _____ are my keys?

2. _____ funny toy is mine?

3. _____ is your birthday party?

4. _____ is Mother coming?

5. _____ was there?

6. _____ is the sky dark?

Draw the other half. Color.

Solve the following problems.

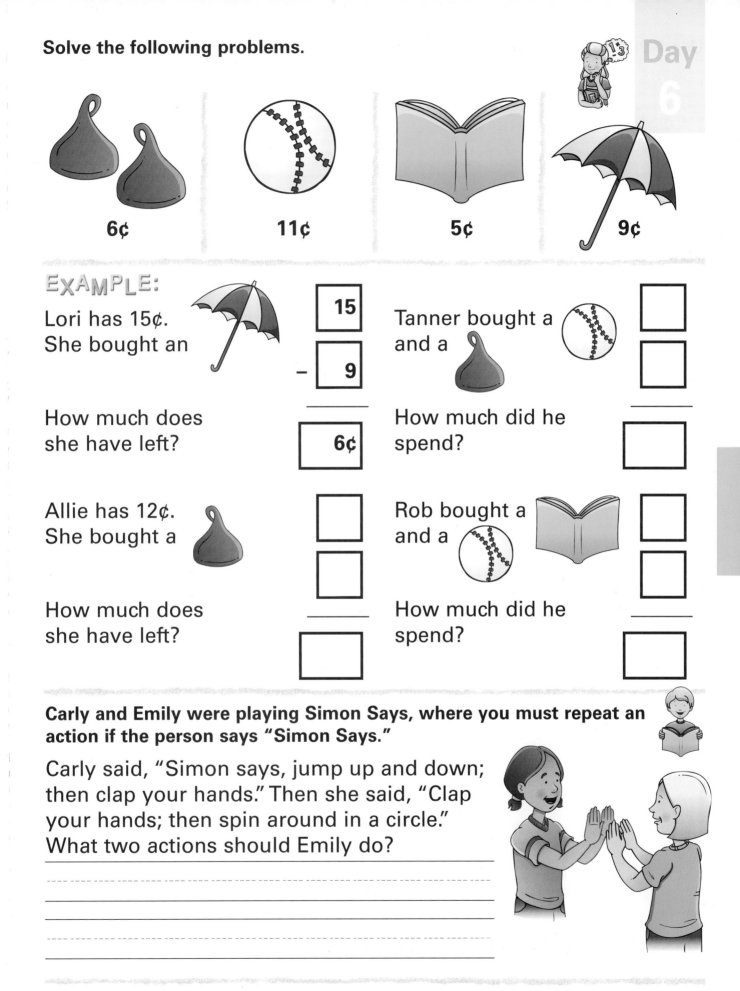

6¢   11¢   5¢   9¢

EXAMPLE:

Lori has 15¢. She bought an [umbrella]

How much does she have left?

15
− 9
____
6¢

Tanner bought a [baseball] and a [candy]

How much did he spend?

Allie has 12¢. She bought a [candy]

How much does she have left?

Rob bought a [baseball] and a [book]

How much did he spend?

Carly and Emily were playing Simon Says, where you must repeat an action if the person says "Simon Says."

Carly said, "Simon says, jump up and down; then clap your hands." Then she said, "Clap your hands; then spin around in a circle." What two actions should Emily do?

_____

_____

_____

Color the correct shape.

Color the
circle purple.

Color the
square blue.

Color the
triangle green.

Color the
rectangle red.

Color the
diamond pink.

Finish the story.

Last night I had the strangest dream. I dreamed that I...

Do a survey with your family and friends to see which flavor of Popsicle is the most popular.

_____ root beer   _____ lime

_____ orange   _____ cherry

_____ banana   _____ grape

                _____ (others not listed)

Graph the results of your survey by placing an X on the coordinates of the number of people who liked each flavor.

Root Beer															
Orange															
Banana															
Lime															
Cherry															
Grape															
Other															
	1	2	3	4	5	6	7	8	9	10	11	12	13	14	15

What is your favorite flavor?   Which flavor was the least popular?

_____   _____

Which flavor was the most popular?

_____

What happens next? Matt and Rob were playing on the swing set when the bell rang. They jumped off the swings, then ran inside to sit at their desks.

Are Matt and Rob at home or at school?

_____

_____

What words helped you to know where _____

_____

they are? _____

Read the story below and then answer the questions.

George lives on a farm. He wakes up early to do chores. George feeds the horses and pigs. He also collects the eggs. Sometimes, he helps his dad milk the cows. His favorite thing to do in the morning is eat breakfast.

1. Where does George live? _____

2. Why does he have to wake up early? _____

3. Name one chore George has to do: _____

4. What is his favorite thing to do in the morning?

_____

Fill in the letters under the picture. Write the words on the correct line to answer the puzzle below. Color each picture the color below its line.

oi

c____ ____n

v____ ____ce

____ ____l

_____   You can put this in your pocket.
yellow

_____   You use this to hum, talk, and laugh.
green

_____   Put this on and no more squeaks!
red

Add.

1.	2	1	4	5	2	4	5
	2	1	4	5	3	3	4
	+ 2	+ 1	+ 4	+ 5	+ 2	+ 0	+ 5

2.	3	6	7	10	8	5	9
	3	6	0	10	3	1	0
	+ 3	+ 6	+ 7	+ 10	+ 2	+ 5	+ 1

Give some facts about you and your family. Draw a picture of your family.

1. I have _____ sisters.
2. I have _____ brothers.
3. My mom's name is
   _____.
4. My dad's name is
   _____.

5. I am _____ years old.
6. We have a pet
   _____.
7. My favorite food is
   _____.
8. My favorite color is
   _____.

What day comes next? Fill in the blanks.

_____ _____

Sunday, _____, _____, Wednesday,

_____ _____

_____, Friday, and _____.

How many days are in a week? _____

Name the days you go to school during the week.

_____ _____

_____, _____, _____

_____, _____, _____

Complete these sentences by unscrambling the words and writing them in the blanks.

1. Matt had a _____ for _____ mother.
   igft   **ihs**

2. The _____ has a broken window.
   acr

3. A bee _____ on _____ flower.
   ats   **hte**

4. My _____ works at the _____.
   add   **tsoer**

5. Sue _____ a _____ dog named Spot.
   sha   **ept**

Add.

1. | 5 | 8 | 3 | 9 | 15 | 10 | 8 |
    |---|---|---|---|----|----|---|
    | + 7 | + 4 | + 7 | + 5 | + 2 | + 6 | + 3 |

Subtract.

2. | 12 | 9 | 11 | 8 | 10 | 6 | 7 |
    |----|---|----|---|----|---|---|
    | − 8 | − 4 | − 7 | − 8 | − 2 | − 2 | − 5 |

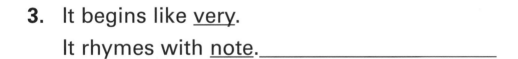

Write the words that match the clues.

EXAMPLE:

1. It begins like <u>stuck</u>.
    It rhymes with <u>late</u>. **state** _____

2. It begins like <u>rip</u>.
    It rhymes with <u>cake</u>. _____

3. It begins like <u>very</u>.
    It rhymes with <u>note</u>. _____

4. It begins like <u>break</u>.
    It rhymes with <u>him</u>. _____

5. It begins like <u>gum</u>.
    It rhymes with <u>late</u>. _____

Read the story below; then answer the questions.

Denise has a box of peaches. She wants to take the peaches home to her mother so her mother can make a peach pie. Denise says, "I love to eat peach pie!"

1. Who has a box of peaches? _____

2. Whom does she want to take the peaches to? _____

3. What does she want her mother to make? _____

4. Denise says, "I love to eat _____ !"

Complete the phrase below. Write at least three complete sentences.

I like myself because I can...

_____

_____

_____

_____

_____

_____

_____

_____

_____

_____

Write the numeral by the number word.

_____ six   _____ nine   _____ four   _____ one

_____ ten   _____ two   _____ three   _____ seven

_____ five   _____ eight   _____ zero   _____ twelve

_____ nineteen   _____ eleven   _____ fourteen

_____ twenty-one   _____ sixteen   _____ eighteen

_____ thirteen   _____ fifteen   _____ seventeen

_____ twenty   _____ twenty-five   _____ thirty

Does the y say (ī) or (ē) in the words below?
Write ī or ē in the boxes.

or

ī   ē

EXAMPLE:

ē				
baby	fly	windy	bunny	fry

shy	family	silly	happy	jelly

cry	my	funny	buy	try

Draw the following.

1. Draw one tree.
2. Draw four flowers.
3. Color one orange butterfly in the tree.
4. Draw a park bench.
5. Draw three pigeons beside the bench.
6. Draw a yellow sun.

Read the story; then answer the questions.

Rob is excited for summer. He wants to do many things. He wants to visit all of the animals at the zoo. He also wants to go camping in the mountains. Rob loves to swim and play with his friends, too.

1. What is Rob excited for? _____

2. What does he want to visit at the zoo? _____

3. Where does he want to go camping? _____

4. What does Rob love to do? _____

   and _____

Use the problems below to work on place value.
Be sure to read before you write.

46 = _____ tens _____ ones

19 = _____ ones _____ tens

84 = _____ tens _____ ones

64 = _____ tens _____ ones

4 tens and 0 ones = _____

1 ten and 1 one = _____

9 ones and 3 tens = _____

1 hundred, 2 tens, and 8 ones = _____

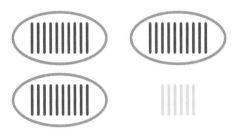

10 10 1 1

_____

Circle the root, or base, word in each of the following words.

EXAMPLE:

1. (run)ning

2. digging

3. stepping

4. hopped

5. slowly

6. careful

7. fastest

8. playful

9. dropped

10. standing

11. boxes

12. catches

13. ripped

14. lovely

15. friendly

16. tallest

17. sickness

18. rabbits

Fill in the circle in front of each correct answer. There may be more than one correct answer in each box.

We can smell
O cakes in the oven.
O cookies on a plate.
O wind blowing the trees.

We can feel
O the cold rain.
O sand on the seashore.
O the night.

We can see
O a sweater on the shelf.
O a pain in our leg.
O a watch on a chain.

We can taste
O the porch swing.
O a green apple.
O a cheese sandwich.

We can feel
O the hot sunshine.
O a cold dish.
O the dog chasing a cat.

We can see
O soldiers marching.
O the weeks.
O a scratch on the table.

We can taste
O a dill pickle.
O popcorn in a dish.
O a cloud in the sky.

We can smell
O a rose on a bush.
O the ticking of a clock.
O dinner cooking.

What would you plant in your garden and why? Draw a picture.

_____
- -
_____
- -
_____
- -
_____
- -
_____

Solve these problems.

Tanner spent 8¢.
Denise spent 2¢.
How much did
they spend
altogether?

Allie has 10 bows.
Lori has 5 bows.
How many bows
do they have?

Rob has 6 fish.
Matt has 2 fish.
How many fish
do they have in
all?

Grayson has 3
balloons. Matt has
8 balloons. How
many balloons do
they have in all?

Study and spell the words in this word list.

brave	glad	stone	fast	crop	lost
slip	slap	last	step	stop	list

Unscramble the words. (Clue: You will find them in your word list.)

psla _____   etsno _____   stal _____

ptos _____   rebav _____   solt _____

porc _____   lgda _____   atsf _____

psil _____   epst _____   stil _____

Read each paragraph and circle the sentence that explains the main idea of the paragraph.

1. Allie's umbrella is old. It has holes in it. The color is faded. It doesn't keep the rain off her.

2. Tabby is a tan and white cat. He has a long, white tail. He lives on a farm in the country. Tabby helps the farmer by catching mice in the barn. He sleeps on soft, green hay.

3. There are big, black clouds in the sky. The wind is blowing, and it is getting cold. It is going to snow.

Find the opposites in the word search box.

1. The opposite of <u>clean</u> is _____.

2. The opposite of <u>night</u> is _____.

3. The opposite of <u>hot</u> is _____.

4. The opposite of <u>light</u> is _____.

5. The opposite of <u>laugh</u> is _____.

6. The opposite of <u>up</u> is _____.

v	d	i	r	t	y	e	h	k
a	b	a	m	c	e	u	d	g
x	c	r	y	o	d	s	a	j
w	l	h	o	l	r	j	y	n
q	a	z	c	d	d	o	w	n
d	a	r	k	b	s	s	l	m
h	r	e	p	s	t	d	j	p

Subtraction. Draw a line between the pairs that have the same answer.

EXAMPLE:

a. 5 – 3 —————— 6 – 4
    3 – 3   9 – 1

b. 8 – 7   9 – 4
    3 – 1   5 – 3

c. 8 – 4   7 – 2
    7 – 5   5 – 1

d. 8 – 2   8 – 3
    9 – 5   7 – 3

e. 10 – 5   7 – 1
    12 – 6   9 – 4
    2 – 0   6 – 0

f. 5 – 5   14 – 7
    12 – 9   8 – 5
    11 – 4   8 – 8

Something is wrong with one word in each sentence. Find the word and correct it!

1. What may i help with?

2. Gve him a brush.

3. You can sti on the chair.

4. Will you miks the paint?

5. Ded you get the pen?

Circle the words that do not belong in the numbered lists below.

EXAMPLE:

1. beans   carrots   corn   (balls)   peas   (books)

2. train   boat   leg   car   dress   jet

3. cat   orange   green   blue   red   five

4. lake   ocean   pond   chair   river   shoe

5. bear   apple   lion   wolf   pillow   tiger

6. Jane   Kathy   Tom   Fred   Jill   Anne

7. park   scared   happy   sad   mad   bee

8. tulip   daffodil   wagon   daisy   basket   rose

A High-Flying Story. This baby eagle needs help. Read the story to learn more about it. Circle the letter of the best answer for each question.

Deke is a baby bald eagle who is learning to fly. It has been a real **hardship** for Deke. He has been practicing for days. **He** just does not seem to be improving.

Getting up in the air was easy. Flying over the plains was no problem. But Deke has trouble flying around things. He does not do well when he **attempts** to land on a certain spot, either. It is hard for Deke to face his friends. Perhaps he should sign up for flying lessons to better his flying skills.

1. The word **hardship** means:
   a. something that is not easy
   b. a boat
   c. a broken wing

2. In the story, the word **He** stands for:
   a. Deke's friend
   b. Deke
   c. the teacher

3. The word **attempts** means:
   a. sings
   b. tries
   c. waits

Help Pocket and his friends find their doggy snacks by drawing a line to match each dog with the correct answer bone.

$$\begin{array}{r} 32 \\ -\ 21 \\ \hline \end{array}$$

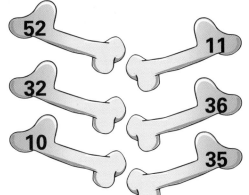

52   11
32   36
10   35

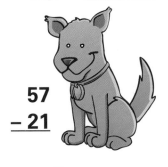

$$\begin{array}{r} 57 \\ -\ 21 \\ \hline \end{array}$$

$$\begin{array}{r} 73 \\ -\ 41 \\ \hline \end{array}$$

$$\begin{array}{r} 20 \\ -\ 10 \\ \hline \end{array}$$

$$\begin{array}{r} 48 \\ -\ 13 \\ \hline \end{array}$$

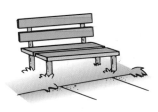

$$\begin{array}{r} 66 \\ -\ 14 \\ \hline \end{array}$$

Circle the letters that spell the ending sounds.

EXAMPLE:

math
$$\begin{array}{r} 12 \\ -\ 2 \\ \hline 10 \end{array}$$

(th) sh ch

th sh ch

th sh ch

th sh ch

th sh ch

th sh ch

th sh ch

th sh ch

Fill in the missing <u>oi</u> or <u>oy</u>; then write the word.

b __ __

_____

s __ __ l

_____

__ __ ster

_____

t __ __

_____

p __ __ nt

_____

Write the correct word in the blank.

1. Grayson _____ a song.   sing   sang

2. Did the bell _____ yet?   ring   rang

3. The bee _____ the king.   stung   sting

4. The waves will _____ the ship.   sank   sink

5. Mom will take a _____ trip.   ship   short

6. I _____ visit Grandma at home.   shack   shall

7. Lori has a _____ on her back.   rash   rush

Finish the chart.

1. O—|—O—|—O—|—O—|—O—|—O—|
    2   4   6   ___   ___   ___

2. O—|—O—|—O—|—O—|—O—|—O—|
    3   ___   9   ___   ___   ___

3. O—|—O—|—O—|—O—|—O—|—O—|
    4   ___   12   ___   ___   ___

4. O—|—O—|—O—|—O—|—O—|—O—|
    5   ___   15   ___   ___   30

Use the Word Study List to do the following activity.

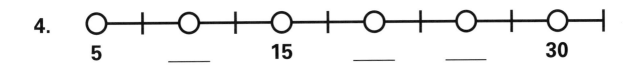

Word Study List
go
me
we
he
no
so
she
be
see
bee

1. Write the word <u>go</u>. Change the beginning letter to make two more words.

    _____ _____ _____

2. Write the words that mean the opposite of <u>yes</u> and <u>stop</u>.

    _____ _____

3. Write <u>she</u>; then write two more words that end the same.

    _____ _____ _____

Fill in the blank with a homophone for the underlined word.
Remember: Homophones sound the same but have different meanings.

made	~~eight~~	sea	through	
wood	right	bee	hear	knot

EXAMPLE:

1. Denise <u>ate</u> ____eight____ pancakes for breakfast.

2. Stay <u>here</u> and you can _____ the music.

3. Can you <u>see</u> the _____ from the top of the hill?

4. <u>Be</u> careful when you catch a _____ .

5. <u>Would</u> you get some _____ for the fire?

6. Did you <u>write</u> the _____ answer?

7. He <u>threw</u> the ball _____ the window.

8. Our <u>maid</u> _____ all the beds.

9. The little girl could <u>not</u> tie a _____ in the rope.

What did you do yesterday?
Write down your activities in the order you did them.

1. _____

2. _____

3. _____

4. _____

5. _____

Read and solve the math problem below.

On July 4th, Rob and his friends went to the parade. It was a hot day. Rob bought five snow cones. He gave one to Grayson, one to Denise, and one to Allie. How many snow cones did Rob have left?

Divide the following compound words.

EXAMPLE: **snow/ball.**

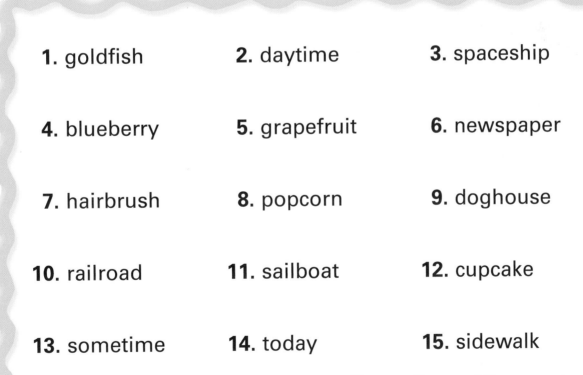

1. goldfish

2. daytime

3. spaceship

4. blueberry

5. grapefruit

6. newspaper

7. hairbrush

8. popcorn

9. doghouse

10. railroad

11. sailboat

12. cupcake

13. sometime

14. today

15. sidewalk

Read and answer the questions.

Years ago, many black-footed ferrets lived in the West. They were wild and free. Their habitat was in the flat grasslands. Their habitat was destroyed by humans.

The ferrets began to vanish. Almost all of them died. Scientists worked to save the ferrets' lives, and now their numbers have increased.

1. Where did the black-footed ferrets live?

_____

2. Who worked to save the ferrets' lives?

_____

3. What happened when the scientists started to work?

_____

How many words can you make using the letters in "camping trip"?

paint

_____

_____

_____

_____

_____

_____

_____

Subtraction.

10	10	10	10	10	10	10
− 2	− 9	− 7	− 1	− 8	− 3	− 4

11	11	11	11	11	11	11
− 2	− 9	− 7	− 1	− 8	− 3	− 5

12	12	12	12	12	12	12
− 2	− 9	− 7	− 1	− 8	− 3	− 5

<u>Synonyms</u> are words that have the same or similar meanings.
<u>Antonyms</u> are words that have opposite meanings.
In each row, underline the synonym and circle the antonym.

1.	big	large	little	dog
2.	fast	slow	car	quick
3.	glad	silly	sad	happy
4.	smile	grin	mouth	frown
5.	day	sunny	night	play

Number the sentences in their correct order.

_____ Lori's friend made a wish and blew out the candles.

_____ Lori put sixteen blue candles on the cake.

_____ Lori made a chocolate cake for her friend.

_____ Lori went to the store and bought a cake mix.

_____ Lori lit the candles with a match.

Draw a picture of the birthday cake Lori made.

Match the sign shapes to the correct answer and then color the signs.

yield
yellow

hospital
blue

railroad
crossing
black/white

phone
blue

stop
red

handicapped
blue

Which balloon has the number described by the tens and ones? Color that balloon. Use the color that is written in each box.

32	23	46	64	81	18
2 tens	3 ones	4 tens	6 ones	1 ten	8 ones
blue		**green**		**purple**	

54	45	93	39	67	76
5 tens	4 ones	3 tens	9 ones	6 tens	7 ones
orange		**black**		**brown**	

One word is spelled wrong in each sentence. Write the correct word from the Word List.

Word List

help

next

leg

pet

net

wet

1. A cat is a good pat. _____

2. She ran to get hlp. _____

3. He sat nekst to her. _____

4. The dog cut his lag. _____

5. The duck got wit. _____

6. The fish is in the nut. _____

71

Read the sentences. Circle the <u>nouns</u> (naming words).

EXAMPLE:

1. The (horse) lost one of his (shoes.)

2. The dog ran after the mailman.

3. A submarine is a boat.

4. The nurse wrote a note to the sick lady.

5. Did you have a sandwich in your lunch?

6. Our teacher showed us a movie about butterflies.

7. The artist drew a beautiful picture of the city.

8. My little sister has a cute teddy bear.

Write the months of the year in the correct order.

March	February	April	August
November	January	May	December
June	September	July	October

1. _____   7. _____

2. _____   8. _____

3. _____   9. _____

4. _____   10. _____

5. _____   11. _____

6. _____   12. _____

1. Circle the odd numbers in each row.

   a. 2   5   7   3   9   4   6   11

   b. 1   10   6   8   12   13   15   2

   c. 5   11   9   13   14   17   19   3

2. Circle the even numbers in each row.

   a. 6   9   2   11   4   7   3   8

   b. 13   8   10   6   12   16   9   5

   c. 14   16   9   11   12   18   7   4

3. Circle the largest number in each set.

   a. 26 or 32   **c.** 51 or 49   **e.** 41 or 14

   b. 19 or 21   **d.** 80 or 60   **f.** 67 or 76

Write the middle consonant of each word below.

pea____uts

se____en

whi____tle

ti____er

flo____er

wi____dow

un____appy

va____uum

Read each sentence. Write the correct word on the line.

or

aw
hawk

au
auto

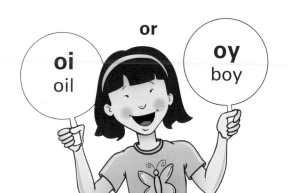

or

oi
oil

oy
boy

1. A dime is a _____.

coin   point   lawn

2. I want to buy my friend a new _____.

boy   toy   claw

3. My cat has one white _____.

paw   saw   car

4. Don has two sons and one _____.

paw   daughter   boil

Invent, design, and describe a new kind of soda pop!

_____
- -
_____
- -
_____
- -
_____
- -
_____
- -
_____
- -
_____

Fill in the blank space with a number to get the answer in the box.

4 − ___ =

3 + ___ =

2 + ___ =

 3

5 + ___ =

2 + ___ =

9 − ___ =

 6

7 + ___ =

___ − 1 =

___ + 2 =

 8

___ − 4 =

8 − ___ =

3 + ___ =

 5

Fill in each blank with the correct contraction.

EXAMPLE:

1. cannot   _can't_

2. I am   _____

3. you are   _____

4. do not   _____

5. he is   _____

6. I will   _____

Write the two words that make up the contraction.

7. didn't   _____

8. isn't   _____

9. you've   _____

10. she's   _____

11. couldn't   _____

12. we're   _____

Fill in the blanks using <u>is</u> or <u>are</u>. On line 9, write a sentence using <u>is</u>. On line 10, write a sentence using <u>are</u>.

1. We _____ going to town tomorrow.

2. The cows _____ in the field.

3. This book _____ not mine.

4. Where _____ a box of chalk?

5. Seals _____ fast swimmers.

6. _____ he going to help you?

7. It _____ very hot outside today.

8. _____ you going to the circus?

9. _____

10. _____

Read the sentences. Put a (.), (!), or (?) at the end of each one.

1. What time do you go to bed___

2. Why did the baby cry___

3. That girl over there is my sister___

4. We do not have our work done___

5. Get out of the way___

6. Are you and I going to the movie___

7. Do monsters have horns on their heads___

8. Look out___That car will run over you___

Super Sediment

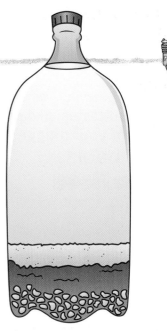

What sinks to the bottom of a creek or a river first—pebbles or particles of dirt? Have you ever thought about it? Try this experiment to find out.

Stuff You Need

funnel
pebbles
soil
soda bottle (2-liter with cap)

paper cup
sand
water

Here's What to Do

1. Use a funnel to pour one paper cup of soil, one of sand, and one of pebbles into the bottle. Pour water into the bottle until it is almost full. Cap it tightly.

2. Shake the bottle until everything is mixed well. Then place the bottle on a shelf. Draw a picture of what you see in your bottle.

3. Watch the particles as they are settling. Come back and check your bottle after 15 or 30 minutes. Check it again in 24 hours.

What's This All About?

We call small bits of rock and soil that get washed into streams and lakes **sediment**. In nature, sediment piles up and forms sedimentary rocks.

In the bottle, you have created a small body of water with lots of sediment. The larger the particle of sediment, the faster it will settle to the bottom of the river or stream. The smaller the particle, the more likely it is to stay in the water longer and settle to the bottom last. In fact, if you were to toss two rocks into a swimming pool, it would be a safe bet that the heavier one would land on the bottom first. Don't try this with large rocks.

More Fun Ideas to Try

1. Find samples of clay, silt, and sand. Fill bottles with each one, add water, shake, and have a race. You can tell how much has settled by how clear the water is. Unless your clay is all in a lump, the samples will settle in the opposite order from how they are listed. Sand will be first, and clay will be last.

Sweet, Sour, Salty, Bitter

Like most people over the age of three, you probably like foods with many different tastes, like pizza and tacos. But did you know you can make a taste map of your tongue?

Stuff You Need

grapefruit rind
lemon
pretzel
sugar cube
water

Here's What to Do

1. Touch a lemon to the very tip of your tongue. Do you taste anything? Don't move your tongue around. Rinse your mouth with water. Touch the lemon to the middle of your tongue and see if you can taste it. Rinse your mouth. Touch the lemon to the sides of your tongue and see if you can taste it.

2. Rinse and repeat with the other items.

What's This All About?

There are four main tastes that we can tell apart: sweet, sour, salty, and bitter. Your tongue is divided into different "taste zones." Each taste zone has its own reserved spot on a certain area of your tongue. By doing this activity, you should be able to discover which part of your tongue detects each kind of taste.

More Fun Ideas to Try

1. Draw a picture of your tongue. Based on your experiments, make a "taste map" of your tongue. Show where you taste salty, sweet, sour, and bitter.

Summer Bridge Activities™

Motivational Calendar

Month

My parents and I decided that if I complete
15 days of **Summer Bridge Activities™** and
read _____ minutes a day, my incentive/reward will be:

Child's Signature _____ Parent's Signature_____

Day 1	☆	📖	_____	Day 9	☆	📖	_____
Day 2	☆	📖	_____	Day 10	☆	📖	_____
Day 3	☆	📖	_____	Day 11	☆	📖	_____
Day 4	☆	📖	_____	Day 12	☆	📖	_____
Day 5	☆	📖	_____	Day 13	☆	📖	_____
Day 6	☆	📖	_____	Day 14	☆	📖	_____
Day 7	☆	📖	_____	Day 15	☆	📖	_____
Day 8	☆	📖	_____				

Child: Color the ☆ for daily activities completed.
Color the 📖 for daily reading completed.

Parent: Initial the _____ when all activities are complete.

Discover Something New!

Fun Activity Ideas to Go Along with Section Three!

1. Play hopscotch, marbles, or jump rope.

2. Visit a fire station.

3. Take a walk around your neighborhood.

4. Name all of the trees and flowers you can.

5. Make up a song.

6. Make a hut out of blankets and chairs.

7. Put a note in a helium balloon and let it go.

8. Start a journal. Write about your favorite vacation memories.

9. Make 3-D nature art. Glue leaves, twigs, dirt, grass, and rocks on paper.

10. Find an ant colony. Spill some food and see what happens.

11. Play charades.

12. Make up a story by drawing pictures.

13. Do something to help the environment. Clean up an area near your house.

14. Weed a row in the garden. Mom will love it!

15. Take a trip to a park.

16. Learn about different road signs.

Subtraction.

A.

15	14	16	17	13
− 4	− 2	− 8	− 3	− 4

B.

10	18	13	11	16
− 4	− 7	− 6	− 9	− 5

C.

17	12	10	18	19
− 8	− 5	− 1	− 4	− 9

Synonyms are words that have the same or nearly the same meaning.
Find a synonym in the train for each of the words below.
Write the word on the line.

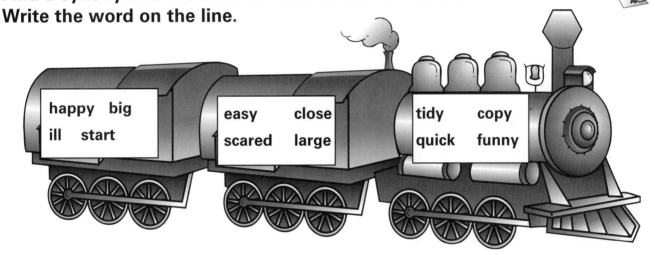

happy   big   ill   start

easy   close   scared   large

tidy   copy   quick   funny

begin _____   afraid _____   trace _____

sick   _____   shut   _____   fast   _____

glad   _____   simple _____   silly   _____

large   _____   big   _____   neat   _____

Unscramble the scrambled word in each sentence and write it correctly.

1. A <u>brzea</u> is an animal in the zoo. _____

2. The robin has <u>nowlf</u> away. _____

3. We mixed flour and eggs in a <u>owlb</u>. _____

4. Button your button and zip your <u>rpzipe</u>. _____

5. A lot of <u>leppeo</u> were at the game. _____

6. We met our new teacher <u>yatdo</u>. _____

7. My old <u>oessh</u> do not fit my feet. _____

8. We made a list of <u>ngtihs</u> to get. _____

9. Jim got <u>irtyd</u> when he fell in the mud. _____

10. <u>eSktri</u> three and you're out. _____

Draw a monster and label the following parts:

stomach, forehead,
tongue, throat,
feet, arms,
eyes, mouth,
legs, nose,
and any other parts
you include.

Addition.

3	6	9	5	4	2
5	4	2	1	3	3
+ 2	+ 3	+ 2	+ 2	+ 4	+ 5

4	7	1	6	2	8
5	2	8	1	3	2
+ 3	+ 1	+ 1	+ 4	+ 2	+ 3

7 + 3 + 1 = _____   8 + 2 + 2 = _____   3 + 5 + 1 = _____

Read the sentences. Find a synonym in the Word Box for each underlined word. Write the new word on the lines. A synonym is a word that has the same or nearly the same meaning as another word.

automobile	small	glad	rush

The baby is very <u>tiny</u>.

_____

- - - - - - - - - - - - - - - -

_____

The <u>car</u> ran out of gas.

_____

- - - - - - - - - - - - - - - -

_____

Susan won, so she was very
<u>happy</u>.

_____

- - - - - - - - - - - - - - - -

_____

My mother was in a big <u>hurry</u>.

_____

- - - - - - - - - - - - - - - -

_____

Make an X by the answers to the questions.

How is a snake like a turtle?	How is a bike like a truck?	How is a sailor like a doctor?

How is a snake like a turtle?

____ 1. They both have shells.

____ 2. They both can be found on land.

____ 3. They are both reptiles.

____ 4. They both fly in the sky.

____ 5. They both have tails.

____ 6. They both eat flies.

How is a bike like a truck?

____ 1. They both have tires.

____ 2. They both need gas.

____ 3. They both can be different colors.

____ 4. They can both be new and shiny.

____ 5. They both have four wheels.

____ 6. They both can go.

How is a sailor like a doctor?

____ 1. They both wear white.

____ 2. They both wear hats.

____ 3. They both work with dogs.

____ 4. They both are people.

____ 5. Their job is to help sick people.

____ 6. They have to work on a ship.

Finish the story.

One day Denise went out to play. Her friend, Lori, was already _____

outside. Lori said to Denise, "Let's go play…"_____

_____

_____

_____

_____

_____

_____

Color in the correct fraction of each picture.

EXAMPLE:

$\frac{1}{2}$ $\frac{1}{3}$ $\frac{1}{4}$

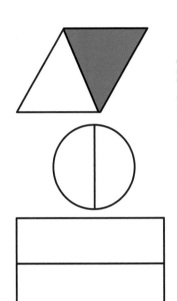
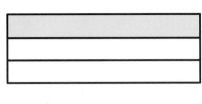
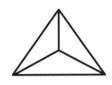
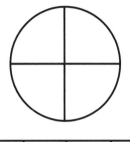

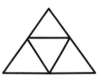
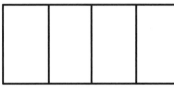

Color the matching bat and ball with the same color.

EXAMPLE:

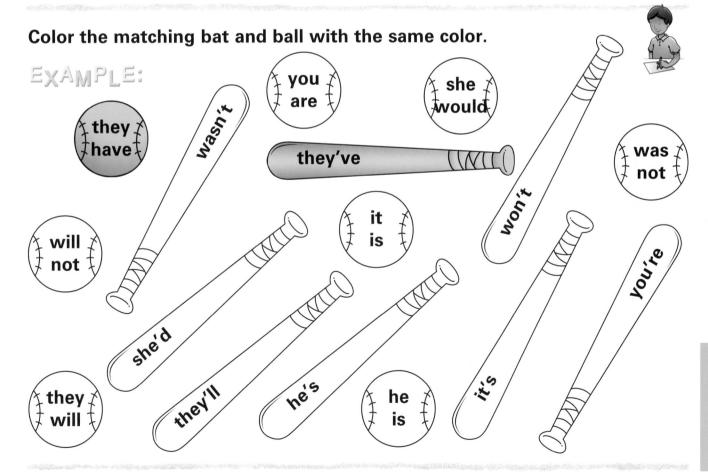

Make up five funny sentences using one word from each column on the hot-air balloon. Do not use any of the words more than once.

children   held
robbers   fed
bugs   followed
bears   found
birds   dropped

1. _____ the balloons.

2. _____ a big truck.

3. _____ the silly cow.

4. _____ the green frog.

5. _____ all the people.

Read the words in the right column. Write the words in alphabetical order in the left column. Draw your favorite animal in the box.

1. _____ pig

2. _____ horse

3. _____ cat

4. _____ frog

5. _____ ant

6. _____ bear

7. _____ giraffe

8. _____ deer

Add or subtract.

11	18	3	10	17	13
+ 7	+ 1	+ 7	− 3	− 2	+ 6

33	64	5	2	12	14
+ 5	− 3	+ 3	+ 4	− 7	− 11

17 + 2 = _____   11 − 3 = _____   13 + 5 = _____

Unscramble the words.

psto _____

sfat _____

ltpae _____

pste _____

gbrni _____

rdnki _____

enwt _____

ithkn _____

oonn _____

ppayh _____

seay _____

dbyo _____

stfri _____

yrc _____

Choose the best adjective from the Word List to complete each sentence.

Word List
funny
six
red
hard
oak
flying
furry

1. His kite got caught in that _____ tree.

2. I can't believe you ate _____ hot dogs!

3. We laughed at the _____ circus clowns.

4. Jackie got a _____ bike for Christmas.

5. My pillow is very _____ and lumpy.

6. The rabbits all had soft and _____ ears.

Circle the main idea of each picture.

1.

The mother pays
Rob and Tanner.

The mother is pretty.

2.

The elves are
wearing green.

The elves are busy
making shoes.

3.

The boys are
wearing masks.

The boys are
standing together.

Color the coins that match the given amount.

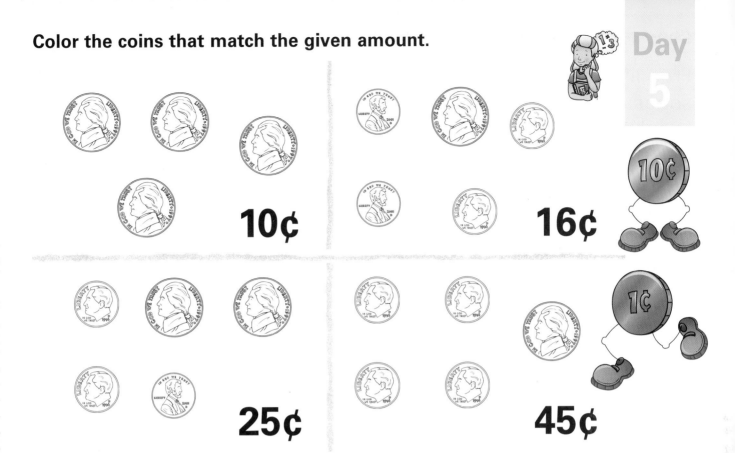

10¢

16¢

25¢

45¢

Match the homophones. <u>Homophones</u> are words that sound the same but have different meanings.

EXAMPLE:

ate	heel	threw	through
cent	sea	pain	pair
knight	night	pear	hear
our	one	know	pane
write	right	here	male
knew	sent	maid	blew
heal	eight	mail	no
see	new	sail	made
won	hour	blue	sale

Story Time. Read the story.

Frog liked to sit on a lily pad in the pond. He liked to sing
songs. He loved to catch bugs, too. His mom told him to be careful,
because his beautiful voice would turn into a croak if he ever sank
into the water. Frog didn't listen. One day, he
ate too many bugs, and the lily pad sank into the
water. When Frog jumped up onto another lily
pad and began to sing, only a croak came out!
Frog shrugged and ate another bug. Yum, yum!

What do you like best about the story?
Why do you think Frog shrugged at the end?

_____

_____

_____

_____

_____

_____

Draw four things that belong in each box.

**Things in
the ocean**

**Things in
the sky**

**Things in
a cave**

Add or subtract.

10	18	7	7	8	6	9
− 4	−14	− 3	+ 5	+ 2	− 4	− 4

11	11	10	9	8	9	7
− 1	+ 8	− 8	+ 8	+ 2	+ 1	− 5

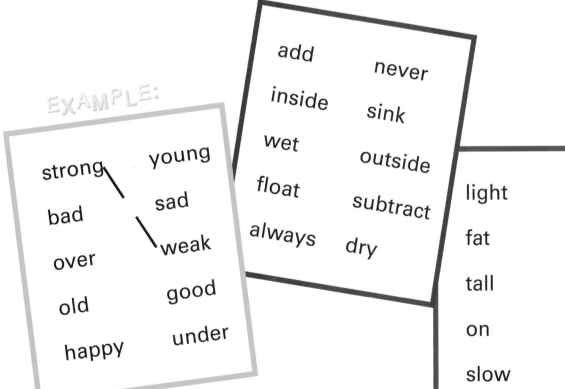

8 + 6 = _____   9 + 3 = _____   4 + 9 = _____

Antonyms. Match the words with opposite meanings.

EXAMPLE:

strong   young
bad   sad
over   weak
old   good
happy   under

add   never
inside   sink
wet   outside
float   subtract
always   dry

light   thin
fat   off
tall   fast
on   dark
slow   short

Read each sentence. Do what it tells you to do. Then put a ✔ in the box to show that you have finished that step.

Let's get ready for lunch.

☐ Draw a plate on the place mat.

☐ Draw a napkin on the left side of the plate.

☐ Draw a fork on the napkin.

☐ Draw a knife and spoon on the right side of the plate.

☐ Draw a glass of purple juice above the napkin.

☐ Draw your favorite lunch.

Enjoy!

Writing.

If I could fly anywhere, I would fly to _____

because... _____

_____

_____

_____

_____

_____

_____

_____

_____

_____

_____

Finish each table.

Add 10	
EXAMPLE: 5	15
8	
7	
9	
3	
4	

Add 8	
2	
6	
4	
7	
3	
5	

Add 6	
10	
6	
8	
7	
4	
5	

Circle the correctly spelled word in each row.

1. ca'nt   can'nt   can't

2. esy   easy   eazy

3. crie   cri   cry

4. kea   key   kee

5. buy   buye   biy

6. lihg   light   ligte

7. allready   already   alredy

8. summ   som   some

9. wonce   onse   once

10. pritty   preety   pretty

11. carry   carey   carrie

12. you're   yure   yo're

13. parte   part   parrt

14. star   stor   starr

15. funy   funny   funnie

16. babie   babey   baby

Circle the correct answer.

1. Another name for <u>boy</u> is: girl   son   funny

2. After seven comes: six   nine   eight

3. I bite with: wheel   teeth   arms

4. A car and truck roll on: with   whip   wheels

5. A farmer grows: ship   wheat   land

6. Your brain helps you: this   thing   think

Do the crossword puzzle.

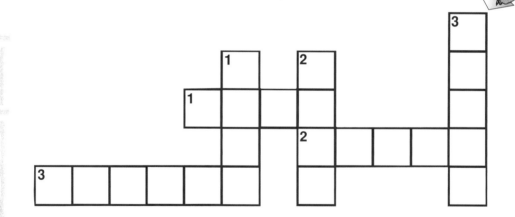

Word List

cent

sent

here

night

write

weight

Down

1. A penny is worth one _____.

2. My friend _____ me a letter.

3. Please _____ your name.

Across

1. Will you please come _____?

2. When the sun goes down, it is _____.

3. The doctor checked my _____.

Make number sentences.
<u>Remember</u>: Use only the numbers in the circles.

EXAMPLE:

13
8   5

__8__ + __5__ = __13__

___ + ___ = ___

___ − ___ = ___

___ − ___ = ___

12
5   7

___ + ___ = ___

___ + ___ = ___

___ − ___ = ___

___ − ___ = ___

14
8   6

___ + ___ = ___

___ + ___ = ___

___ − ___ = ___

___ − ___ = ___

6   9
15

___ + ___ = ___

___ + ___ = ___

___ − ___ = ___

___ − ___ = ___

Put the words under the correct sound–picture.

Word List

| long o (ō) nose | short o (ŏ) pop |

bone	fox
those	coat
log	rock
drove	top
job	rope

long o (ō) nose

1. ___
2. ___
3. ___
4. ___
5. ___

short o (ŏ) pop

1. ___
2. ___
3. ___
4. ___
5. ___

Read the sentences. Circle and write the action verb in each sentence.

EXAMPLE:

1. The chicken (ran) away. __ran_____

2. Judy cut her finger with the knife. _____

3. A kangaroo can hop very fast. _____

4. I like to swim in our pool._____

5. Ted and Sid will chop some wood. _____

6. That kitten likes to climb trees. _____

7. We will eat dinner at six o'clock._____

8. The baby was yawning._____

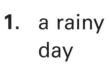

Draw a face beside each statement that shows how it makes you feel.

1. a rainy day

2. fighting with a friend

3. chocolate cake

4. birthday presents

5. playing soccer

6. going to Grandmother's

Addition.

3	3	6	2	4	5
2	4	1	2	3	4
+ 1	+ 2	+ 2	+ 3	+ 3	+ 6

1	6	7	4	5	4
3	3	2	5	2	4
+ 2	+ 1	+ 1	+ 2	+ 3	+ 1

Write soft <u>c</u> words under <u>pencil</u>. Write hard <u>c</u> words under <u>candy</u>.

grocery	cattle	cement	corn	price
cake	cellar	crib	grace	cow

pencil   candy

1. _____   1. _____

2. _____   2. _____

3. _____   3. _____

4. _____   4. _____

5. _____   5. _____

Unscramble the sentences. Write the words in the correct order.

1. sun shine will today The.

2. mile today I a walked.

3. house We painted our.

4. Mother knit will I something for.

Write a letter. Ask someone to a silly picnic.

Start your letter with "Dear _____,"
End your letter with "Yours truly, _____."

Color the shape that matches the description.

10	**23**	**17**	**57**
2 tens	3 ones	5 tens	7 ones
green		purple	

52	**59**	**23**	**32**
5 tens	2 ones	2 tens	3 ones
yellow		orange	

39	**29**	**10**	**20**
3 tens	9 ones	1 ten	0 ones
red		blue	

Write each word under the correct sound–picture.

tower	blow	mow	clown	elbow	crown
flown	bowls	how	frown	own	brown

cow   pillow

Draw a line to the right word.

EXAMPLE:

1. Something near you is   clock

2. Something that tells time is a   bird

3. A time of day is   babies

4. A crow is a kind of   snoop

5. A place where fish live is an   close

6. Pork is a kind of   dusk

7. Chicks, ducklings, and fawns are kinds of   aquarium

8. A shop is a kind of   strike

9. To hit something is to   store

10. To look in someone else's things is to   meat

Write as many words as you can that describe...

ice cream

watermelon

Subtract.

57	68	96	57	38	59
− 32	− 44	− 92	− 43	− 3	− 45

83	75	48	95	68	39	89
− 62	− 20	− 4	− 31	− 26	− 10	− 53

19	24	52	63	76	88	90
− 3	− 11	− 31	− 41	− 22	− 44	− 30

Write in the name of each picture and color.

s o ___ ___

g r ___ ___ s

___ ___ s h

s h ___ ___ t

___ ___ o v e

g a t ___

Complete the sentences by writing nouns that make sense on the lines.

1. The _____ went to the beach.

2. A nurse works in a _____.

3. A _____ ran when the alligator moved.

4. My _____ put the _____ in a jar.

5. A _____ tastes very sweet.

6. The _____ made a lot of _____.

Before school starts again, I want to...

_____

_____

_____

_____

_____

_____

_____

_____

_____

_____

_____

_____

_____

Finish each table.

EXAMPLE:

subtract 5	
9	4
5	
7	
10	
11	
8	

subtract 3	
10	
9	
7	
8	
6	
11	

subtract 2	
11	
7	
9	
5	
8	
6	

Circle the correct r-controlled vowel.

EXAMPLE:

 bird

ir   or   ar

ur   or   ar

ir   or   ar

ar   ur   or

ur   or   ar

ir   or   ar

ir   or   ar

ir   et   ar

er   or   ar

er   ur   ar

ir   or   ar

er   or   ar

Complete the riddles.

1. I am rather tiny. I have wings and buzz around.
    I can be a real pest at picnics. I am a _____.

2. I was just born. My mother and father feed me and keep me
    dry. I cry and sleep, but I cannot walk. I am a _____.

3. I am made of metal and am quite little. I can lock things up
    and open them, too! I am a _____.

4. I like to sing. I lay eggs. I like to eat bugs and worms.
    I am a _____.

Number the sentences in each group 1–4 to show the correct order.

_____ Doug chased lightning bugs.

_____ The jar broke, and the bugs flew away.

_____ Doug caught two lightning bugs.

_____ Doug put the lightning bugs in a jar.

_____ Nick came home from school.

_____ Nick made a sandwich.

_____ Nick ate a sandwich.

_____ Nick went to the kitchen.

Math. Below are two mileage maps. Use them to answer the questions.

How many miles is it from Salt Lake City to Bountiful? _____ miles

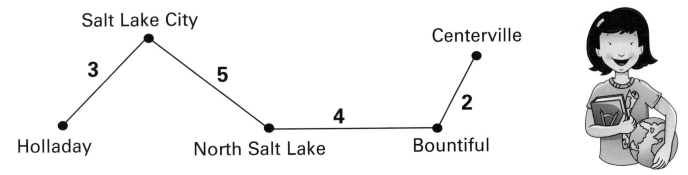

How many miles is it from Provo to Pleasant Grove? _____ miles

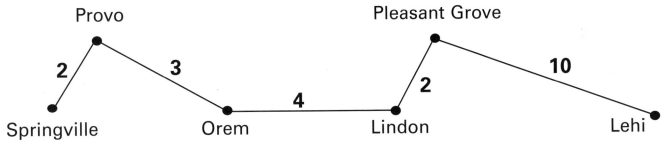

Read the sentences. Is the underlined word in each sentence spelled right or wrong? Circle the correct answer.

		EXAMPLE:	right	(wrong)
1.	Jane is a very <u>brav</u> girl.		right	wrong
2.	The flag is red, white, and <u>bloo</u>.		right	wrong
3.	Those girls are in my <u>class</u>.		right	wrong
4.	Mike is a very <u>helpfull</u> friend.		right	wrong
5.	I remembered to turn off the <u>light</u>.		right	wrong
6.	This candy is sticky <u>stuf</u>.		right	wrong
7.	Is <u>shee</u> coming with us?		right	wrong
8.	Don't <u>lose</u> your boots.		right	wrong

105

Noisy or quiet? Put an <u>N</u> in front of things that are noisy and a <u>Q</u> in front of things that are quiet. Draw a noisy picture and a quiet picture.

___ **1.** A butterfly flying through the air.

___ **2.** A cook using a mixer to make a cake.

___ **3.** Popcorn popping on the stove.

___ **4.** A dress hanging up to dry.

___ **5.** A child reading to herself.

___ **6.** Ice cream melting in the sun.

___ **7.** A cat and dog fighting in the driveway.

___ **8.** A band marching in a parade.

Noisy

Quiet

Homonyms. The following words sound and are spelled the same but have two different meanings. Write two sentences using the different meanings.

> **bat:** a wooden stick that is used to hit a ball
> a small animal that flies at night

_____

_____

_____

> **spring:** the season of the year between winter and summer
> to jump or bounce into the air

_____

_____

_____

Add or subtract.

24	16	28	37	42	12
+ 12	− 0	− 14	− 26	+ 27	+ 11

87¢	79¢	3	15¢	97	40
− 16¢	− 54¢	+ 13	+ 24¢	− 64	+ 40

12	18	41	66	13	30
40	20	6	22	22	12
+ 62	+ 11	+ 32	+ 11	+ 24	+ 10

Circle either g or j below each word to show which sound the g makes.

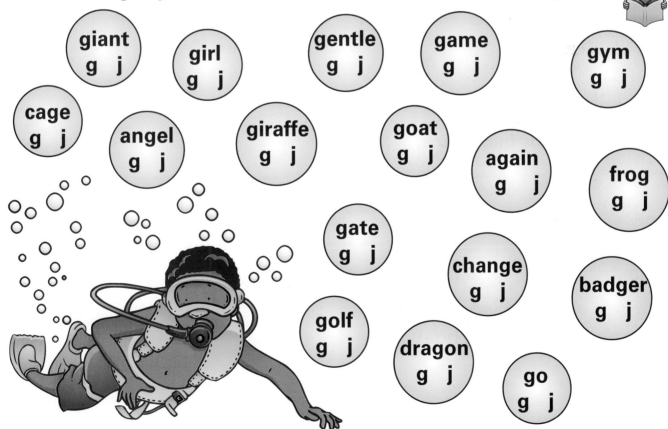

giant
g   j

girl
g   j

gentle
g   j

game
g   j

gym
g   j

cage
g   j

angel
g   j

giraffe
g   j

goat
g   j

again
g   j

frog
g   j

gate
g   j

change
g   j

badger
g   j

golf
g   j

dragon
g   j

go
g   j

Answer the riddles. Write the correct short <u>a</u> (ă) word on the line. Then draw a picture of your answer in the box.

The mother of baby kittens
is a ___ ___ ___.

To play baseball you need a ball and
___ ___ ___.

When we cross the street, hold my ___ ___ ___ ___.   '

Match the words that rhyme.

EXAMPLE:

goat	tree	shoe	hair
last	band	chair	two
bee	boat	mean	rain
sand	fast	train	bean

Write the number of gum balls in each picture.

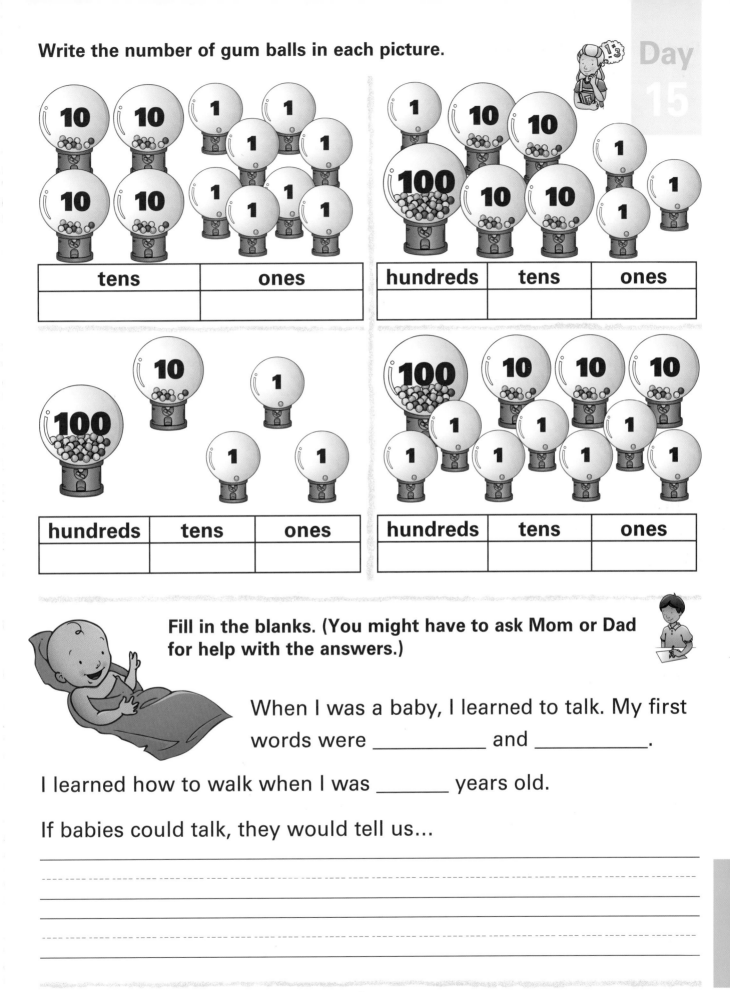

tens	ones

hundreds	tens	ones

hundreds	tens	ones

hundreds	tens	ones

Fill in the blanks. (You might have to ask Mom or Dad for help with the answers.)

When I was a baby, I learned to talk. My first words were _____ and _____.

I learned how to walk when I was _____ years old.

If babies could talk, they would tell us...

_____
_____
_____
_____

End each sentence with the correct mark. Use a (.), (!), or (?).

Allie went to the zoo ____

The tigers scared Allie ____

Do you like the zoo ____

Rob visited a farm ____

Pigs are huge and messy ____

What is your favorite animal ____

Write a sentence or two.

"I can be safe this summer by…" (For example: staying away from rivers, not getting sunburned, keeping my bike out of the road when I ride, etc.)

_____

_____

_____

_____

_____

_____

_____

_____

Catching Ice Cubes

In winter, people use salt to melt ice on sidewalks. You can use salt to catch an ice cube with a piece of string.

Stuff You Need

ice cube
salt
string (12 inches)

Here's What to Do

1. Try to catch the ice cube with just a 12-inch piece of string and nothing else. You can't tie the string around the ice cube. Can you do it?

2. Now, lay the string on the ice cube and sprinkle a little salt on the string. Count to three and slowly lift up the string. Like magic, the ice cube is now attached!

What's This All About?

As the salt touches the water layer on the surface of the ice cube, the water dissolves the salt.

The salt uses energy to dissolve. Whenever energy is used, heat is released. This makes the water freeze again, which attaches the string to the ice. This type of reaction also happens when you fill an ice tray with hot water and put it in the freezer. It will actually freeze faster than an ice tray full of cold water! Try it and see.

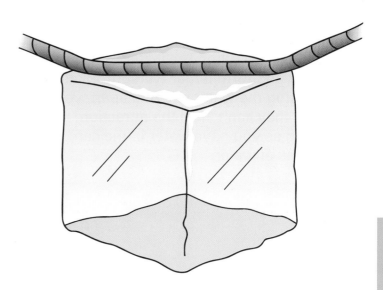

Pinching Water

Could you hold two streams of water together or separate two streams of water that had been flowing together? You'd probably have to be pretty powerful! Or would you?

Stuff You Need

adult
hammer
masking tape
nail (8- or 16-penny)
soup can (empty)
water

Here's What to Do

1. Ask an adult to use the hammer and nail to punch two small holes in the lower section of the can. The holes should be very close to the bottom and half an inch apart. Look at the picture if you have any questions. Put a piece of tape over the holes.

2. Fill the can with water. Take the can outside or hold it over a sink. Remove the tape. Which direction does the water shoot?

3. Try pinching the two streams together; then try to split the two streams apart.

What's This All About?

When you pinch the streams of water together, the water molecules are attracted to each other. The water molecules act like magnets—they attract each other and form larger water droplets.

By flicking the water streams apart, you push the streams far enough away that they can't "feel the attraction." So they stay separate.

As long as you have water in the can, you will be able to pinch and split the streams of water.

Answer Pages

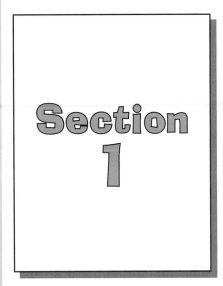

Section 1

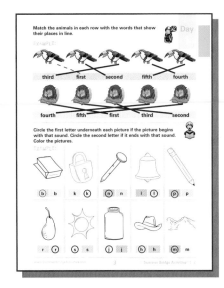

Page 3

Page 4

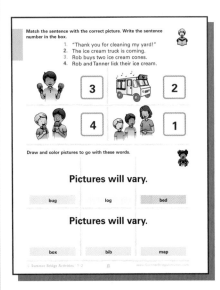

Page 5

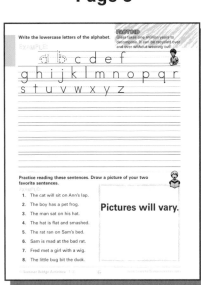

Page 6

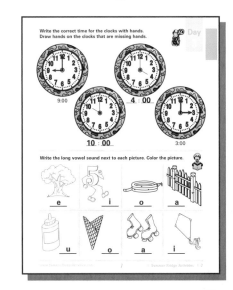

Page 7

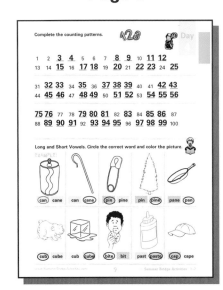

Page 8

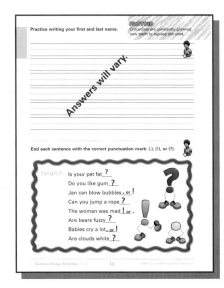

Page 9

Page 10

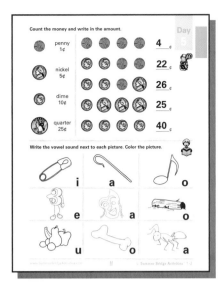

Page 11

Count the money and write in the amount.

Day 5

penny 1¢		4 ¢
nickel 5¢		22 ¢
dime 10¢		26 ¢
quarter 25¢		25 ¢
		40 ¢

Write the vowel sound next to each picture. Color the picture.

i   a   o
e   a   o
u   o   a

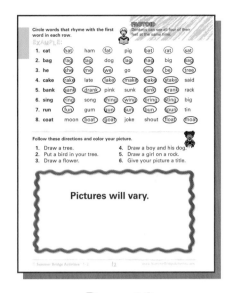

Page 12

Circle words that rhyme with the first word in each row.

FACTOID Donkeys can see all four of their feet at the same time.

EXAMPLE:
1. cat — hat, ham, fat, pig, bat, rat, sat
2. bag — rag, tag, dog, lag, nag, big, sag
3. he — she, me, we, go, see, be, tree
4. cake — rake, late, cake, make, take, stake, said
5. bank — sank, drank, pink, sunk, tank, crank, rack
6. sing — ring, song, thing, wing, bring, sting, big
7. run — fun, gum, gun, sun, bun, spun, tin
8. coat — moon, boat, goat, joke, shout, float, moat

Follow these directions and color your picture.
1. Draw a tree.
2. Put a bird in your tree.
3. Draw a flower.
4. Draw a boy and his dog.
5. Draw a girl on a rock.
6. Give your picture a title.

Pictures will vary.

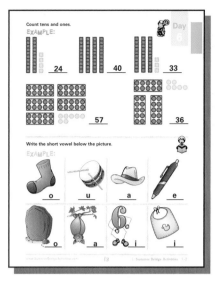

Page 13

Count tens and ones.

Day 6

EXAMPLE:
24   40   33
57   36

Write the short vowel below the picture.

EXAMPLE:
o   u   a   e
o   a   i   i

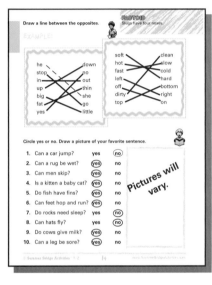

Page 14

Draw a line between the opposites.

FACTOID Sloths have four noses.

EXAMPLE:
he — down
stop — no
in — out
up — thin
big — she
fat — go
yes — little

soft — clean
hot — slow
fast — cold
left — hard
off — bottom
dirty — right
top — on

Circle yes or no. Draw a picture of your favorite sentence.
1. Can a car jump? yes **no**
2. Can a rug be wet? **yes** no
3. Can men skip? **yes** no
4. Is a kitten a baby cat? **yes** no
5. Do fish have fins? **yes** no
6. Can feet hop and run? **yes** no
7. Do rocks need sleep? yes **no**
8. Can hats fly? yes **no**
9. Do cows give milk? **yes** no
10. Can a leg be sore? **yes** no

Pictures will vary.

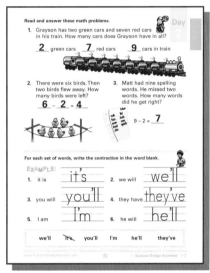

Page 15

Read and answer these math problems.

Day 7

1. Grayson has two green cars and seven red cars in his train. How many cars does Grayson have in all?
2 green cars   7 red cars   9 cars in train

2. There were six birds. Then two birds flew away. How many birds were left?
6 - 2 = 4

3. Matt had nine spelling words. He missed two words. How many words did he get right?
9 - 2 = 7

For each set of words, write the contraction in the word blank.
EXAMPLE:
1. it is — it's
2. we will — we'll
3. you will — you'll
4. they have — they've
5. I am — I'm
6. he will — he'll

we'll   it's   you'll   I'm   he'll   they've

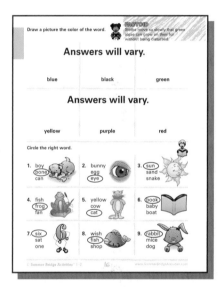

Page 16

Draw a picture the color of the word.

FACTOID Sloths move so slowly that green algae can grow on their fur without being disturbed.

Answers will vary.

blue   black   green

Answers will vary.

yellow   purple   red

Circle the right word.
1. boy, **bone**, can
2. bunny, egg, **eye**
3. **sun**, sand, snake
4. fish, **frog**, fan
5. yellow, cow, **cat**
6. **book**, baby, boat
7. **six**, sat, one
8. wish, **fish**, shop
9. **rabbit**, mice, dog

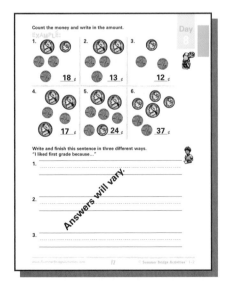

Page 17

Count the money and write in the amount.

Day 8

EXAMPLE:
1. 18 ¢   2. 13 ¢   3. 12 ¢
4. 17 ¢   5. 24 ¢   6. 37 ¢

Write and finish this sentence in three different ways.
"I liked first grade because…"
1.
2.
3.

Answers will vary.

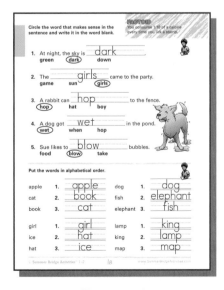

Page 18

Circle the word that makes sense in the sentence and write it in the word blank.

FACTOID You consume 1/10 of a calorie every time you lick a stamp.

1. At night, the sky is **dark**.
green, **dark**, down
2. The **girls** came to the party.
game, sun, **girls**
3. A rabbit can **hop** to the fence.
hop, hat, boy
4. A dog got **wet** in the pond.
wet, when, hop
5. Sue likes to **blow** bubbles.
food, **blow**, take

Put the words in alphabetical order.
apple   1. apple   dog   1. dog
cat   2. book   fish   2. elephant
book   3. cat   elephant 3. fish
girl   1. girl   lamp   1. king
ice   2. hat   king   2. lamp
hat   3. ice   map   3. map

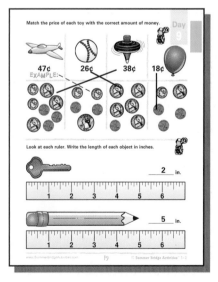

Page 19

Match the price of each toy with the correct amount of money.

Day 9

47¢   26¢   38¢   18¢
EXAMPLE:

Look at each ruler. Write the length of each object in inches.
2 in.
5 in.

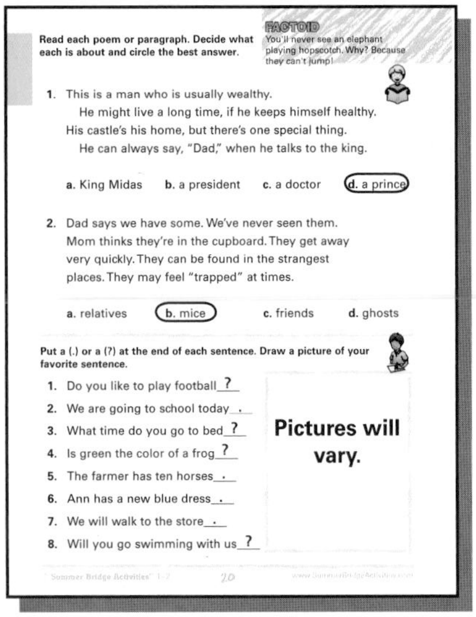
Read each poem or paragraph. Decide what each is about and circle the best answer.

FACTOID: You'll never see an elephant playing hopscotch. Why? Because they can't jump!

1. This is a man who is usually wealthy.
He might live a long time, if he keeps himself healthy.
His castle's his home, but there's one special thing.
He can always say, "Dad," when he talks to the king.

a. King Midas b. a president c. a doctor (d. a prince)

2. Dad says we have some. We've never seen them. Mom thinks they're in the cupboard. They get away very quickly. They can be found in the strangest places. They may feel "trapped" at times.

a. relatives (b. mice) c. friends d. ghosts

Put a (.) or a (?) at the end of each sentence. Draw a picture of your favorite sentence.

1. Do you like to play football ?
2. We are going to school today .
3. What time do you go to bed ?
4. Is green the color of a frog ?
5. The farmer has ten horses .
6. Ann has a new blue dress .
7. We will walk to the store .
8. Will you go swimming with us ?

Pictures will vary.

Page 20

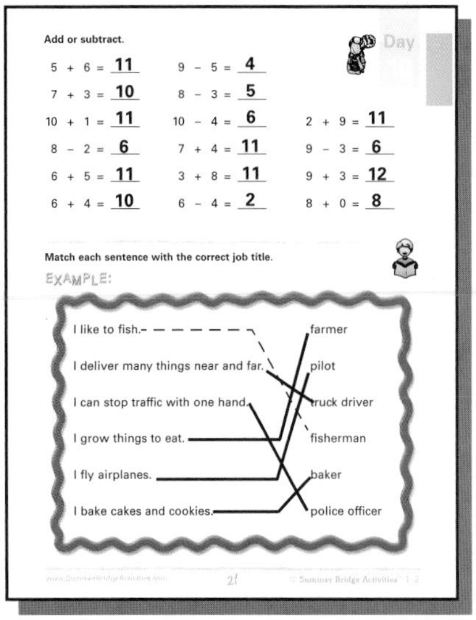
Add or subtract.

5 + 6 = 11	9 − 5 = 4	
7 + 3 = 10	8 − 3 = 5	
10 + 1 = 11	10 − 4 = 6	2 + 9 = 11
8 − 2 = 6	7 + 4 = 11	9 − 3 = 6
6 + 5 = 11	3 + 8 = 11	9 + 3 = 12
6 + 4 = 10	6 − 4 = 2	8 + 0 = 8

Match each sentence with the correct job title.

EXAMPLE:

I like to fish. — fisherman
I deliver many things near and far. — truck driver
I can stop traffic with one hand. — police officer
I grow things to eat. — farmer
I fly airplanes. — pilot
I bake cakes and cookies. — baker

Page 21

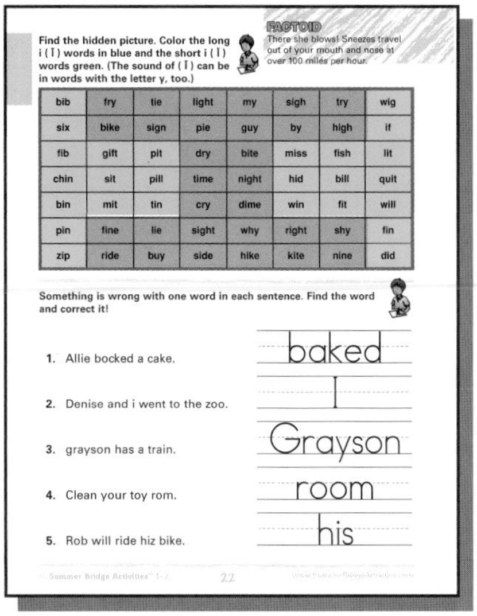
Find the hidden picture. Color the long i (ī) words in blue and the short i (ĭ) words green. (The sound of (ī) can be in words with the letter y, too.)

FACTOID: There she blows! Sneezes travel out of your mouth and nose at over 100 miles per hour.

bib	fry	tie	light	my	sigh	try	wig
six	bike	sign	pie	guy	by	high	if
fib	gift	pit	dry	bite	miss	fish	lit
chin	sit	pill	time	night	hid	bill	quit
bin	mit	tin	cry	dime	win	fit	will
pin	fine	lie	sight	why	right	shy	fin
zip	ride	buy	side	hike	kite	nine	did

Something is wrong with one word in each sentence. Find the word and correct it!

1. Allie bocked a cake. — baked
2. Denise and i went to the zoo. — I
3. grayson has a train. — Grayson
4. Clean your toy rom. — room
5. Rob will ride hiz bike. — his

Page 22

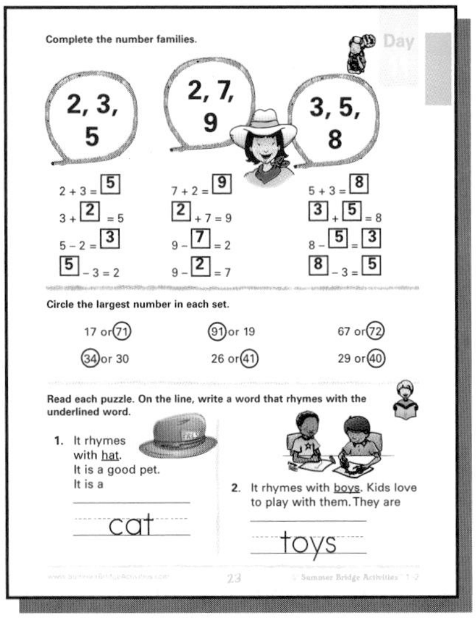
Complete the number families.

2, 3, 5: 2 + 3 = 5; 3 + 2 = 5; 5 − 2 = 3; 5 − 3 = 2
2, 7, 9: 7 + 2 = 9; 2 + 7 = 9; 9 − 7 = 2; 9 − 2 = 7
3, 5, 8: 5 + 3 = 8; 3 + 5 = 8; 8 − 5 = 3; 8 − 3 = 5

Circle the largest number in each set.

17 or (71) (91) or 19 67 or (72)
(34) or 30 26 or (41) 29 or (40)

Read each puzzle. On the line, write a word that rhymes with the underlined word.

1. It rhymes with hat. It is a good pet. It is a cat
2. It rhymes with boys. Kids love to play with them. They are toys

Page 23

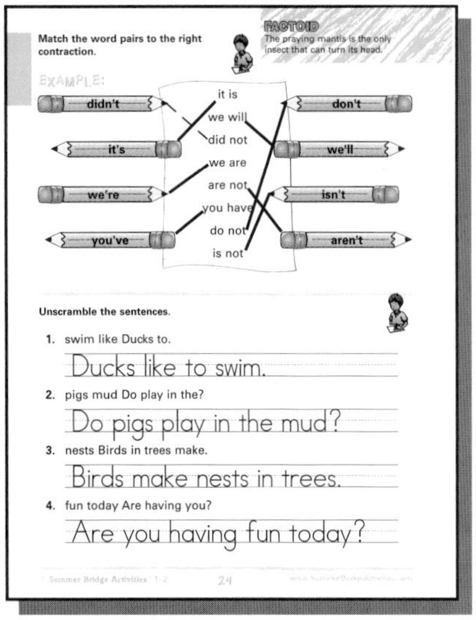
Match the word pairs to the right contraction.

FACTOID: The praying mantis is the only insect that can turn its head.

EXAMPLE:

didn't — did not
it's — it is
we're — we are
you've — you have
don't — do not
we'll — we will
isn't — is not
aren't — are not

Unscramble the sentences.

1. swim like Ducks to.
Ducks like to swim.
2. pigs mud Do play in the?
Do pigs play in the mud?
3. nests Birds in trees make.
Birds make nests in trees.
4. fun today Are having you?
Are you having fun today?

Page 24

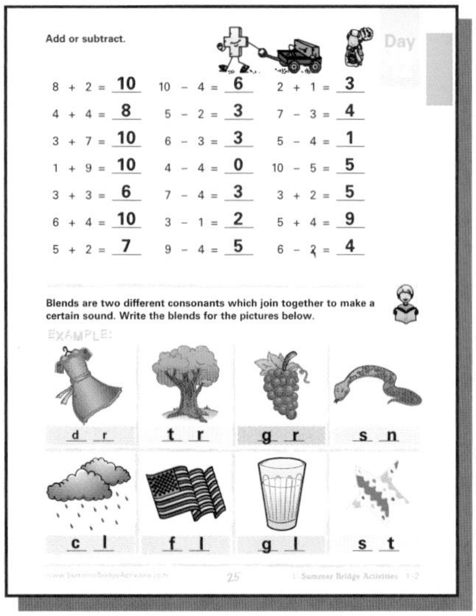
Add or subtract.

8 + 2 = 10	10 − 4 = 6	2 + 1 = 3
4 + 4 = 8	5 − 2 = 3	7 − 3 = 4
3 + 7 = 10	6 − 3 = 3	5 − 4 = 1
1 + 9 = 10	4 − 4 = 0	10 − 5 = 5
3 + 3 = 6	7 − 4 = 3	3 + 2 = 5
6 + 4 = 10	3 − 1 = 2	5 + 4 = 9
5 + 2 = 7	9 − 4 = 5	6 − 2 = 4

Blends are two different consonants which join together to make a certain sound. Write the blends for the pictures below.

EXAMPLE:

d r t r g r s n
c l f l g l s t

Page 25

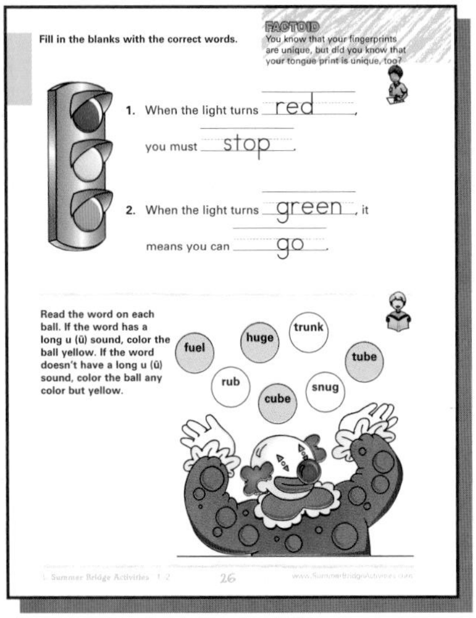
Fill in the blanks with the correct words.

FACTOID: You know that your fingerprints are unique, but did you know that your tongue print is unique, too?

1. When the light turns red, you must stop.
2. When the light turns green, it means you can go.

Read the word on each ball. If the word has a long u (ū) sound, color the ball yellow. If the word doesn't have a long u (ū) sound, color the ball any color but yellow.

fuel, huge, trunk, tube, rub, cube, snug

Page 26

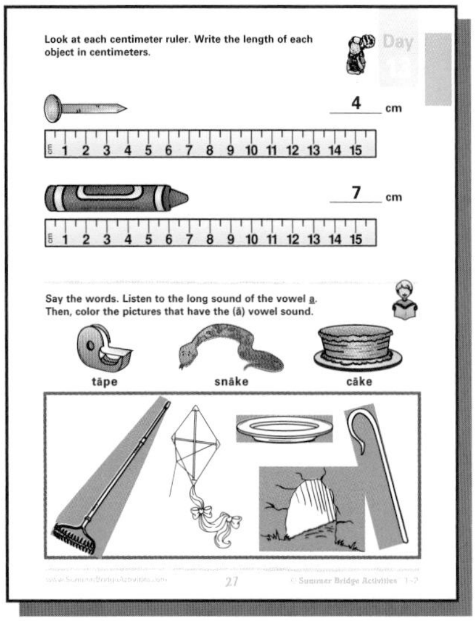
Look at each centimeter ruler. Write the length of each object in centimeters.

4 cm

7 cm

Say the words. Listen to the long sound of the vowel a. Then, color the pictures that have the (ā) vowel sound.

tāpe snāke cāke

Page 27

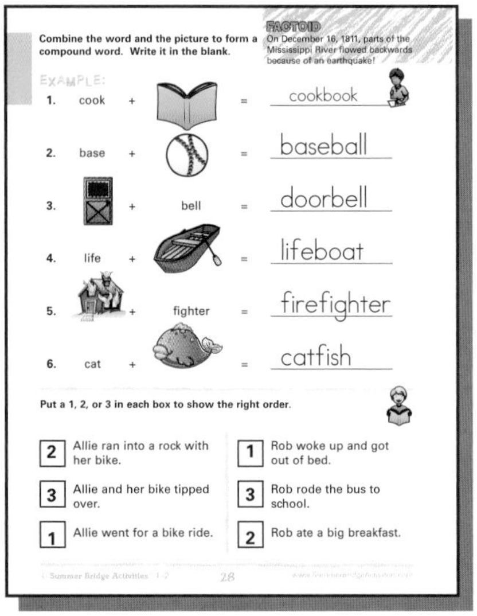
Combine the word and the picture to form a compound word. Write it in the blank.

FACTOID: On December 16, 1811, parts of the Mississippi River flowed backwards because of an earthquake!

EXAMPLE:

1. cook + = cookbook
2. base + = baseball
3. + bell = doorbell
4. life + = lifeboat
5. + fighter = firefighter
6. cat + = catfish

Put a 1, 2, or 3 in each box to show the right order.

2 Allie ran into a rock with her bike.
3 Allie and her bike tipped over.
1 Allie went for a bike ride.

1 Rob woke up and got out of bed.
3 Rob rode the bus to school.
2 Rob ate a big breakfast.

Page 28

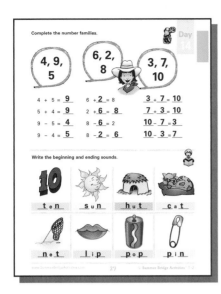

Page 29

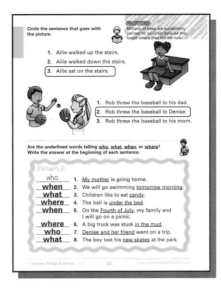

Page 30

Page 31

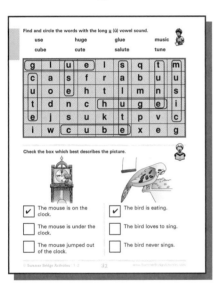

Page 32

Section 2

Page 37

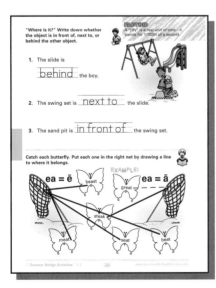

Page 38

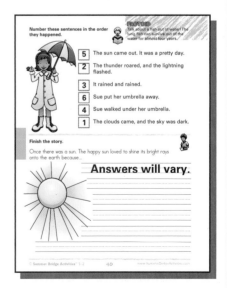

Page 39

Page 40

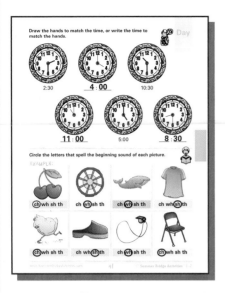

Page 41

Draw the hands to match the time, or write the time to match the hands.

2:30   4:00   10:30

11:00   5:00   8:30

Circle the letters that spell the beginning sound of each picture.

EXAMPLE:
(ch) wh sh th   ch (wh) sh th   ch (wh) sh th   ch wh (sh) th

ch (wh) sh th   ch wh (sh) th   ch (wh) sh th   (ch) wh sh th

Page 42

Read and decide.
One day, a man went on a hunt. He hunted for a long time. At the end of the day, he was very happy. What do you think the man found? Did he find something to eat? Did he find something pretty? Did he find something funny? Decide what the man found and draw a picture of it!

Pictures will vary.

Put the following words in alphabetical order.

he, up, fat, little, big, stop, and, out, slow, go

1. and   6. little
2. big   7. out
3. fat   8. slow
4. go   9. stop
5. he   10. up

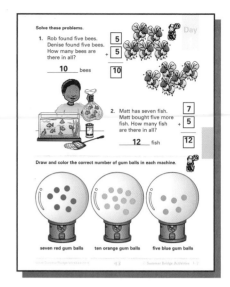

Page 43

Solve these problems.

1. Rob found five bees. Denise found five bees. How many bees are there in all?
   10 bees

   5 + 5 = 10

2. Matt has seven fish. Matt bought five more fish. How many fish are there in all?
   12 fish

   7 + 5 = 12

Draw and color the correct number of gum balls in each machine.

seven red gum balls   ten orange gum balls   five blue gum balls

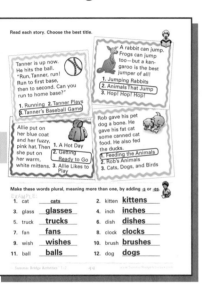

Page 44

Read each story. Choose the best title.

Tanner is up now. He hits the ball. "Run, Tanner, run! Run to first base, then to second. Can you run to home base?"
1. Running 2. Tanner Plays **3. Tanner's Baseball Game**

A rabbit can jump. Frogs can jump too—but a kangaroo is the best jumper of all!
1. Jumping Rabbits **2. Animals That Jump** 3. Hop! Hop! Hop!

Allie put on her blue coat and her fuzzy, pink hat. Then she put on her warm, white mittens.
1. A Hot Day **2. Getting Ready to Go** 3. Allie Likes to Play

Rob gave his pet dog a bone. He gave his fat cat some canned cat food. He also fed the ducks.
1. Feeding the Animals 2. Rob's Animals 3. Cats, Dogs, and Birds

Make these words plural, meaning more than one, by adding -s or -es.

EXAMPLE:
1. cat — cats
2. kitten — kittens
3. glass — glasses
4. inch — inches
5. truck — trucks
6. dish — dishes
7. fan — fans
8. clock — clocks
9. wish — wishes
10. brush — brushes
11. ball — balls
12. dog — dogs

Page 45

Subtract and fill in the answers on the outer circle.

EXAMPLE:

Circle and write the word that goes with each picture.

glove / glue — **glove**
flower / flag — **flower**
flashlight / fly — **flashlight**

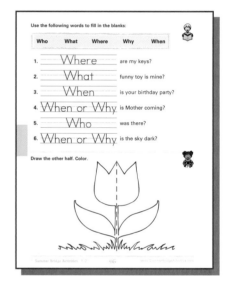

Page 46

Use the following words to fill in the blanks:

Who   What   Where   Why   When

1. Where are my keys?
2. What funny toy is mine?
3. When is your birthday party?
4. When or Why is Mother coming?
5. Who was there?
6. When or Why is the sky dark?

Draw the other half. Color.

Page 47

Solve the following problems.

6¢   11¢   5¢   9¢

EXAMPLE:
Lori has 15¢. She bought an [umbrella]
15 - 9
How much does she have left? 6¢

Allie has 12¢. She bought a [kiss]
12 - 6
How much does she have left? 6¢

Tanner bought a [umbrella] and a [kiss]
11 + 6
How much did he spend? 17¢

Rob bought a [book] and a [ball]
5 + 11
How much did he spend? 16¢

Carly and Emily were playing Simon Says, where you must repeat an action if the person says "Simon Says."

Carly said, "Simon says, jump up and down; then clap your hands." Then she said, "Clap your hands; then spin around in a circle." What two actions should Emily do?

jump up and down
clap your hands

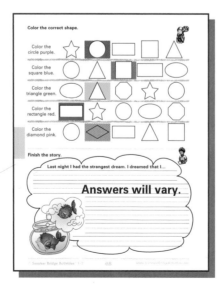

Page 48

Color the correct shape.

Color the circle purple.
Color the square blue.
Color the triangle green.
Color the rectangle red.
Color the diamond pink.

Finish the story.

Last night I had the strangest dream. I dreamed that I...

Answers will vary.

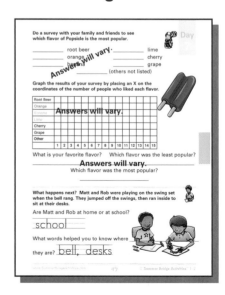

Page 49

Do a survey with your family and friends to see which flavor of Popsicle is the most popular.

____ root beer   ____ lime
____ orange   ____ cherry
____ grape
(others not listed)

Answers will vary.

Graph the results of your survey by placing an X on the coordinates of the number of people who liked each flavor.

Root Beer / Orange / Lime / Cherry / Grape / Other
1 2 3 4 5 6 7 8 9 10 11 12 13 14 15

Answers will vary.

What is your favorite flavor?   Which flavor was the least popular?
Answers will vary.
Which flavor was the most popular?

What happens next? Matt and Rob were playing on the swing set when the bell rang. They jumped off the swings, then ran inside to sit at their desks.

Are Matt and Rob at home or at school?
school

What words helped you to know where they are? bell, desks

Page 50

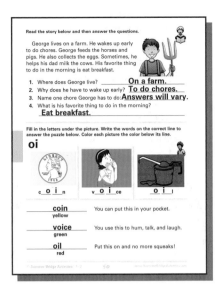

Read the story below and then answer the questions.

George lives on a farm. He wakes up early to do chores. George feeds the horses and pigs. He also collects the eggs. Sometimes, he helps his dad milk the cows. His favorite thing to do in the morning is eat breakfast.

1. Where does George live? **On a farm.**
2. Why does he have to wake up early? **To do chores.**
3. Name one chore George has to do? **Answers will vary.**
4. What is his favorite thing to do in the morning? **Eat breakfast.**

Fill in the letters under the picture. Write the words on the correct line to answer the puzzle below. Color each picture the color below its line.

oi

c_o_i_n   v_o_i_ce   o_i_l

coin (yellow) — You can put this in your pocket.

voice (green) — You use this to hum, talk, and laugh.

oil (red) — Put this on and no more squeaks!

Page 51

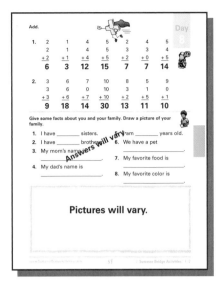

Add.

1.
2	1	4	5	2	4	5
+2	+1	+4	+5	+5	+0	+5
6	3	12	15	7	7	14

2.
3	6	7	10	5	8	9
+3	+6	+7	+10	+2	+5	+1
9	18	14	30	13	11	10

Give some facts about you and your family. Draw a picture of your family.

1. I have _____ sisters.
2. I have _____ brothers.
3. My mom's name is _____
4. My dad's name is _____

5. I am _____ years old.
6. We have a pet _____
7. My favorite food is _____
8. My favorite color is _____

Answers will vary.

Pictures will vary.

Page 52

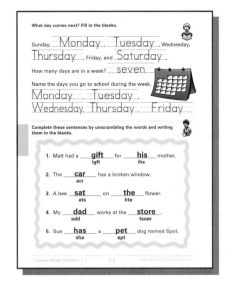

What day comes next? Fill in the blanks.

Sunday, **Monday**, **Tuesday**, Wednesday, **Thursday**, Friday, and **Saturday**

How many days are in a week? **seven**

Name the days you go to school during the week.

Monday, **Tuesday**, **Wednesday**, **Thursday**, **Friday**

Complete these sentences by unscrambling the words and writing them in the blanks.

1. Matt had a **gift** (igft) for **his** (ihs) mother.
2. The **car** (acr) has a broken window.
3. A bee **sat** (ats) on **the** (hte) flower.
4. My **dad** (add) works at the **store** (tsoer).
5. Sue **has** (sha) a **pet** (ept) dog named Spot.

Page 53

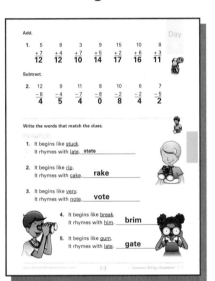

Add.

1.
5	8	3	9	15	10	8
+7	+4	+7	+5	+2	+6	+3
12	12	10	14	17	16	11

Subtract.

2.
12	9	11	8	10	6	7
-8	-4	-7	-8	-2	-2	-5
4	5	4	0	8	4	2

Write the words that match the clues.

EXAMPLE:

1. It begins like stuck. It rhymes with late. **state**
2. It begins like rip. It rhymes with cake. **rake**
3. It begins like very. It rhymes with note. **vote**
4. It begins like break. It rhymes with him. **brim**
5. It begins like gum. It rhymes with late. **gate**

Page 54

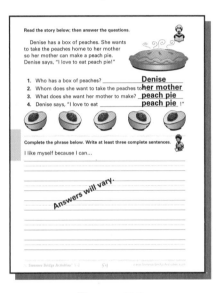

Read the story below; then answer the questions.

Denise has a box of peaches. She wants to take the peaches home to her mother so her mother can make a peach pie. Denise says, "I love to eat peach pie!"

1. Who has a box of peaches? **Denise**
2. Whom does she want to take the peaches to? **her mother**
3. What does she want her mother to make? **peach pie**
4. Denise says, "I love to eat **peach pie** !"

Complete the phrase below. Write at least three complete sentences.

I like myself because I can...

Answers will vary.

Page 55

Write the numeral by the number word.

6 six   **9** nine   **4** four   **1** one
10 ten   **2** two   **3** three   **7** seven
5 five   **8** eight   **0** zero   **12** twelve

19 nineteen   **11** eleven   **14** fourteen
21 twenty-one   **16** sixteen   **18** eighteen
13 thirteen   **15** fifteen   **17** seventeen
20 twenty   **25** twenty-five   **30** thirty

Does the _y_ say ($\bar{\imath}$) or ($\bar{e}$) in the words below? Write $\bar{\imath}$ or $\bar{e}$ in the boxes.

EXAMPLE:
$\bar{e}$ bab_y_ $\bar{\imath}$ fl_y_ $\bar{e}$ wind_y_ $\bar{e}$ bunn_y_ $\bar{\imath}$ fr_y_

$\bar{\imath}$ sh_y_ $\bar{e}$ famil_y_ $\bar{e}$ sill_y_ $\bar{e}$ happ_y_ $\bar{e}$ jell_y_

$\bar{\imath}$ cr_y_ $\bar{\imath}$ m_y_ $\bar{e}$ funn_y_ $\bar{\imath}$ bu_y_ $\bar{\imath}$ tr_y_

Page 56

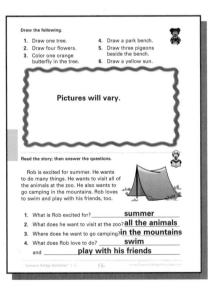

Draw the following.

1. Draw one tree.
2. Draw four flowers.
3. Color one orange butterfly in the tree.
4. Draw a park bench.
5. Draw three pigeons beside the bench.
6. Draw a yellow sun.

Pictures will vary.

Read the story; then answer the questions.

Rob is excited for summer. He wants to do many things. He wants to visit all of the animals at the zoo. He also wants to go camping in the mountains. Rob loves to swim and play with his friends, too.

1. What is Rob excited for? **summer**
2. What does he want to visit at the zoo? **all the animals**
3. Where does he want to go camping? **in the mountains**
4. What does Rob love to do? **swim** and **play with his friends**

Page 57

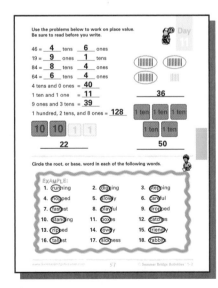

Use the problems below to work on place value. Be sure to read before you write.

46 = **4** tens **6** ones
19 = **9** ones **1** tens
84 = **8** tens **4** ones
64 = **6** tens **4** ones
4 tens and 0 ones = **40**
1 ten and 1 one = **11**
9 ones and 3 tens = **39**
1 hundred, 2 tens, and 8 ones = **128**

| 10 | 10 | 1 | 1 |
22

| 1 ten | 1 ten | 1 ten |
36

| 1 ten | 1 ten |
50

Circle the root, or base, word in each of the following words.

EXAMPLE:
1. running
2. digging
3. stepping
4. mopped
5. slowly
6. careful
7. fastest
8. playful
9. dropped
10. standing
11. boxes
12. catches
13. ripped
14. lovely
15. friendly
16. tallest
17. sickness
18. rabbit

Page 58

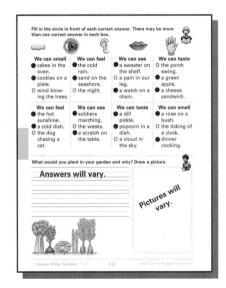

Fill in the circle in front of each correct answer. There may be more than one correct answer in each box.

We can smell
● cakes in the oven.
● cookies on a plate.
○ wind blowing the trees.

We can see
● the cold rain.
● sand on the seashore.
○ the night.

We can feel
● a sweater on the shelf.
○ a pain in our leg.
● a watch on a chain.

We can taste
○ the porch swing.
● a green apple.
● a cheese sandwich.

We can feel
● the hot sunshine.
● a cold dish.
○ the dog chasing a cat.

We can see
● soldiers marching.
○ the weeks.
● a scratch on the table.

We can taste
● a dill pickle.
● popcorn in a dish.
○ a cloud in the sky.

We can smell
● a rose on a bush.
○ the ticking of a clock.
● dinner cooking.

What would you plant in your garden and why? Draw a picture.

Answers will vary.

Pictures will vary.

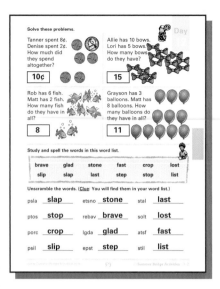

Page 59

Solve these problems.

Tanner spent 8¢. Denise spent 2¢. How much did they spend altogether?

10¢

Allie has 10 bows. Lori has 5 bows. How many bows do they have?

15

Rob has 6 fish. Matt has 2 fish. How many fish do they have in all?

8

Grayson has 3 balloons. Matt has 8 balloons. How many balloons do they have in all?

11

Study and spell the words in this word list.

| brave | glad | stone | fast | crop | lost |
| slip | slap | last | step | stop | list |

Unscramble the words. (Clue: You will find them in your word list.)

psla **slap**   etsno **stone**   stal **last**

ptos **stop**   rebav **brave**   solt **lost**

porc **crop**   lgda **glad**   atsf **fast**

psil **slip**   epst **step**   stil **list**

Page 60

Read each paragraph and circle the sentence that explains the main idea of the paragraph.

1. [Allie's umbrella is old.] It has holes in it. The color is faded. It doesn't keep the rain off her.

2. [Tabby is a tan and white cat.] He has a long, white tail. He lives on a farm in the country. Tabby helps the farmer by catching mice in the barn. He sleeps on soft, green hay.

3. There are big, black clouds in the sky. The wind is blowing, and it is getting cold. [It is going to snow.]

Find the opposites in the word search box.

1. The opposite of clean is **dirty**.
2. The opposite of night is **day**.
3. The opposite of hot is **cold**.
4. The opposite of light is **dark**.
5. The opposite of laugh is **cry**.
6. The opposite of up is **down**.

v	d	i	r	t	y	e	h	k
a	b	a	m	c	e	u	d	g
x	c	r	y	o	d	s	a	j
w	l	h	o	l	r	j	y	n
q	a	z	c	d	d	o	w	n
d	a	r	k	b	s	s	l	m
h	r	e	p	s	t	d	j	p

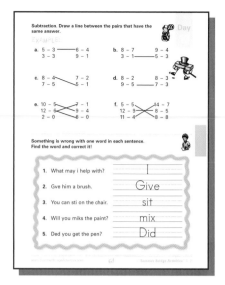

Page 61

Subtraction. Draw a line between the pairs that have the same answer.

a. 5 – 3 —— 6 – 4   b. 8 – 7   9 – 4
    4 – 2   9 – 1   3 – 1   5 – 3

c. 8 – 4   7 – 2   d. 8 – 2   8 – 5
    7 – 5   5 – 1   9 – 5   7 – 3

e. 10 – 5   7 – 1   f. 5 – 5   14 – 7
    12 – 6   9 – 4   12 – 9   8 – 5
    2 – 0   6 – 0   11 – 4   8 – 8

Something is wrong with one word in each sentence. Find the word and correct it!

1. What may i help with? **I**
2. Gve him a brush. **Give**
3. You can sti on the chair. **sit**
4. Will you miks the paint? **mix**
5. Ded you get the pen? **Did**

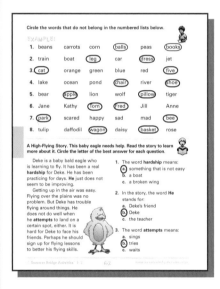

Page 62

Circle the words that do not belong in the numbered lists below.

EXAMPLE:
1. beans   carrots   corn   (balls)   peas   (books)
2. train   boat   (leg)   car   (dress)   jet
3. (cat)   orange   green   blue   red   (five)
4. lake   ocean   pond   (chair)   river   (shoe)
5. bear   (apple)   lion   wolf   (pillow)   tiger
6. Jane   Kathy   (Tom)   (Fred)   Jill   Anne
7. (park)   scared   happy   sad   mad   (bee)
8. tulip   daffodil   (wagon)   daisy   (basket)   rose

A High-Flying Story. This baby eagle needs help. Read the story to learn more about it. Circle the letter of the best answer for each question.

Deke is a baby bald eagle who is learning to fly. It has been a real **hardship** for Deke. He has been practicing for days. **He** just does not seem to be improving.

Getting up in the air was easy. Flying over the plains was no problem. But Deke has trouble flying around things. He does not do well when he **attempts** to land on a certain spot, either. It is hard for Deke to face his friends. Perhaps he should sign up for flying lessons to better his flying skills.

1. The word **hardship** means:
   a. something that is not easy
   b. a boat
   c. a broken wing

2. In the story, the word **He** stands for:
   a. Deke's friend
   b. Deke
   c. the teacher

3. The word **attempts** means:
   a. sings
   b. tries
   c. waits

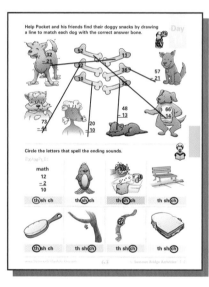

Page 63

Help Pocket and his friends find their doggy snacks by drawing a line to match each dog with the correct answer bone.

Circle the letters that spell the ending sounds.

EXAMPLE:
math
12
– 2
10

th sh ch   th sh ch   th sh ch   th sh ch

th sh ch   th sh ch   th sh ch   th sh ch

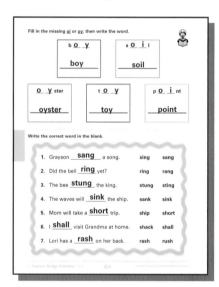

Page 64

Fill in the missing oi or oy; then write the word.

b **o y**   s **o i** l
boy   **soil**

o y ster   t **o y**   p **o i** nt
oyster   **toy**   **point**

Write the correct word in the blank.

1. Grayson **sang** a song.   sing   sang
2. Did the bell **ring** yet?   ring   rang
3. The bee **stung** the king.   stung   sting
4. The waves will **sink** the ship.   sank   sink
5. Mom will take a **short** trip.   ship   short
6. I **shall** visit Grandma at home.   shack   shall
7. Lori has a **rash** on her back.   rash   rush

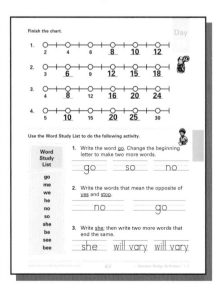

Page 65

Finish the chart.

1. 2   4   6   **8**   **10**   **12**
2. 3   **6**   9   **12**   **15**   **18**
3. 4   **8**   12   **16**   **20**   **24**
4. 5   **10**   15   **20**   **25**   30

Use the Word Study List to do the following activity.

| Word Study List |
| go |
| me |
| we |
| he |
| no |
| so |
| she |
| be |
| see |
| bee |

1. Write the word go. Change the beginning letter to make two more words.
go   **so**   **no**

2. Write the words that mean the opposite of yes and stop.
no   **go**

3. Write she; then write two more words that end the same.
she   **will vary**   **will vary**

Page 66

Fill in the blank with a homophone for the underlined word. Remember: Homophones sound the same but have different meanings.

| made | eight | sea | through |
| wood | right | bee | hear | knot |

EXAMPLE:
1. Denise ate **eight** pancakes for breakfast.
2. Stay here and you can **hear** the music.
3. Can you see the **sea** from the top of the hill?
4. Be careful when you catch a **bee**.
5. Would you get some **wood** for the fire?
6. Did you write the **right** answer?
7. He threw the ball **through** the window.
8. Our maid **made** all the beds.
9. The little girl could not tie a **knot** in the rope.

What did you do yesterday? Write down your activities in the order you did them.

1. _Answers will vary._
2.
3.
4.
5.

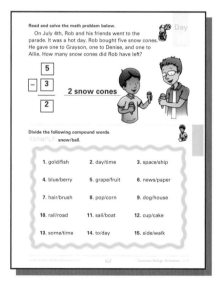

Page 67

Read and solve the math problem below.

On July 4th, Rob and his friends went to the parade. It was a hot day. Rob bought five snow cones. He gave one to Grayson, one to Denise, and one to Allie. How many snow cones did Rob have left?

5 – **3** = **2**   2 snow cones

Divide the following compound words.
EXAMPLE: snow/ball.

1. gold/fish   2. day/time   3. space/ship
4. blue/berry   5. grape/fruit   6. news/paper
7. hair/brush   8. pop/corn   9. dog/house
10. rail/road   11. sail/boat   12. cup/cake
13. some/time   14. to/day   15. side/walk

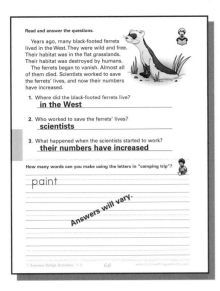

Read and answer the questions.

Years ago, many black-footed ferrets lived in the West. They were wild and free. Their habitat was in the flat grasslands. Their habitat was destroyed by humans.

The ferrets began to vanish. Almost all of them died. Scientists worked to save the ferrets' lives, and now their numbers have increased.

1. Where did the black-footed ferrets live?
   __in the West__

2. Who worked to save the ferrets' lives?
   __scientists__

3. What happened when the scientists started to work?
   __their numbers have increased__

How many words can you make using the letters in "camping trip"?

paint

Answers will vary.

Page 68

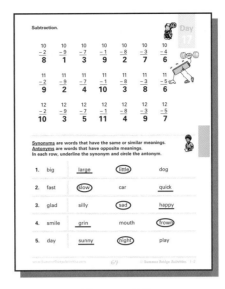

Subtraction.

10 −2 **8**	10 −9 **1**	10 −7 **3**	10 −1 **9**	10 −8 **2**	10 −3 **7**	10 −4 **6**
11 −2 **9**	11 −9 **2**	11 −7 **4**	11 −1 **10**	11 −8 **3**	11 −3 **8**	11 −5 **6**
12 −2 **10**	12 −9 **3**	12 −7 **5**	12 −1 **11**	12 −8 **4**	12 −3 **9**	12 −5 **7**

Synonyms are words that have the same or similar meanings.
Antonyms are words that have opposite meanings.
In each row, underline the synonym and circle the antonym.

1. big — large — (little) — dog
2. fast — (slow) — car — quick
3. glad — silly — (sad) — happy
4. smile — grin — mouth — (frown)
5. day — sunny — (night) — play

Page 69

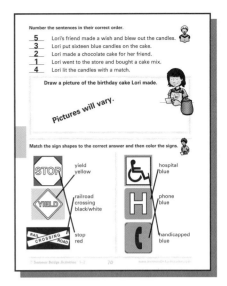

Number the sentences in their correct order.

5 Lori's friend made a wish and blew out the candles.
3 Lori put sixteen blue candles on the cake.
2 Lori made a chocolate cake for her friend.
1 Lori went to the store and bought a cake mix.
4 Lori lit the candles with a match.

Draw a picture of the birthday cake Lori made.

Pictures will vary.

Match the sign shapes to the correct answer and then color the signs.

STOP — yield / yellow
YIELD — railroad crossing / black/white
RAIL CROSSING ROAD — stop / red
H — hospital / blue
phone / blue
handicapped / blue

Page 70

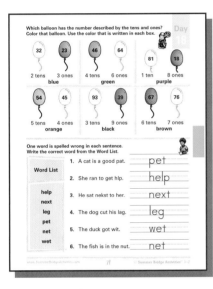

Which balloon has the number described by the tens and ones? Color that balloon. Use the color that is written in each box.

32 **23** — 2 tens 3 ones — **blue**
46 64 — 4 tens 6 ones — **green**
81 **18** — 1 ten 8 ones — **purple**
54 **45** — 5 tens 4 ones — **orange**
93 **39** — 3 tens 9 ones — **black**
67 76 — 6 tens 7 ones — **brown**

One word is spelled wrong in each sentence. Write the correct word from the Word List.

Word List
help
next
leg
pet
net
wet

1. A cat is a good pat. — **pet**
2. She ran to get hlp. — **help**
3. He sat nekst to her. — **next**
4. The dog cut his lag. — **leg**
5. The duck got wit. — **wet**
6. The fish is in the nut. — **net**

Page 71

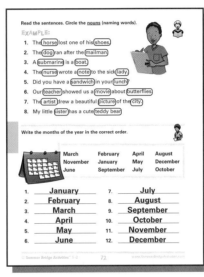

Read the sentences. Circle the nouns (naming words).

EXAMPLE:
1. The (horse) lost one of his (shoes).
2. The (dog) ran after the (mailman).
3. A (submarine) is a (boat).
4. The (nurse) wrote a (note) to the sick (lady).
5. Did you have a (sandwich) in your (lunch)?
6. Our (teacher) showed us a (movie) about (butterflies).
7. The (artist) drew a beautiful (picture) of the (city).
8. My little (sister) has a cute (teddy bear).

Write the months of the year in the correct order.

March November June / February January September / April May July / August December October

1. **January**
2. **February**
3. **March**
4. **April**
5. **May**
6. **June**
7. **July**
8. **August**
9. **September**
10. **October**
11. **November**
12. **December**

Page 72

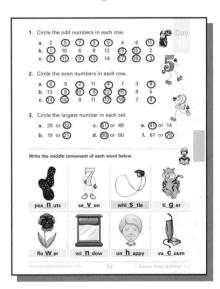

1. Circle the odd numbers in each row.
   a. 2 (5) (7) (3) (9) 4 6 (11)
   b. (1) 10 6 (13) 2 12 (9) (3)
   c. (5) (11) (9) (3) (13) 14 (17) (19) (3)

2. Circle the even numbers in each row.
   a. (6) 9 (2) 11 (4) 7 (8) 3
   b. (8) (3) (10) (6) 9 11 (12) (4)
   c. (14) (16) 9 11 (12) (18) 7 (4)

3. Circle the largest number in each set.
   a. 26 or (32) c. (51) or 49 e. (41) or 14
   b. 19 or (21) d. (80) or 60 f. 67 or (76)

Write the middle consonant of each word below.

pea__n__uts se__v__en whi__s__tle ti__g__er
flo__w__er wi__n__dow un__h__appy va__c__uum

Page 73

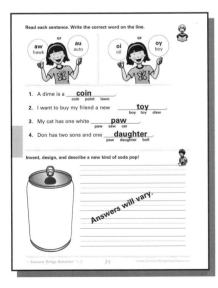

Read each sentence. Write the correct word on the line.

aw / hawk — or — au / auto
oi / oil — or — oy / boy

1. A dime is a __coin__
   coin point lawn
2. I want to buy my friend a new __toy__
   boy toy claw
3. My cat has one white __paw__
   paw saw car
4. Don has two sons and one __daughter__
   paw daughter boil

Invent, design, and describe a new kind of soda pop!

Answers will vary.

Page 74

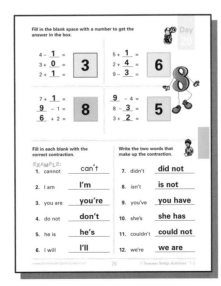

Fill in the blank space with a number to get the answer in the box.

4 − **1** =
3 + **0** = **3**
2 + **1** =

5 + **1** =
2 + **4** = **6**
9 − **3** =

7 + **1** =
9 − **1** = **8**
6 + **2** =

9 − 4 =
8 − **3** = **5**
3 + **2** =

Fill in each blank with the correct contraction.

EXAMPLE:
1. cannot — **can't**
2. I am — **I'm**
3. you are — **you're**
4. do not — **don't**
5. he is — **he's**
6. I will — **I'll**

Write the two words that make up the contraction.

7. didn't — **did not**
8. isn't — **is not**
9. you've — **you have**
10. she's — **she has**
11. couldn't — **could not**
12. we're — **we are**

Page 75

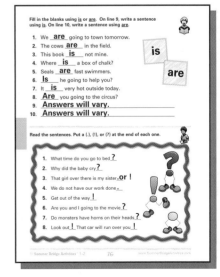

Fill in the blanks using is or are. On line 9, write a sentence using is. On line 10, write a sentence using are.

1. We **are** going to town tomorrow.
2. The cows **are** in the field.
3. This book **is** not mine.
4. Where **is** a box of chalk?
5. Seals **are** fast swimmers.
6. **Is** he going to help you?
7. It **is** very hot outside today.
8. **Are** you going to the circus?
9. **Answers will vary.**
10. **Answers will vary.**

Read the sentences. Put a (.), (!), or (?) at the end of each one.

1. What time do you go to bed **?**
2. Why did the baby cry **?**
3. That girl over there is my sister **. or !**
4. We do not have our work done **.**
5. Get out of the way **!**
6. Are you and I going to the movie **?**
7. Do monsters have horns on their heads **?**
8. Look out! That car will run over you **!**

Page 76

Section 3

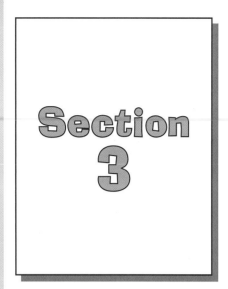

© Summer Bridge Activities™ 1–2   122   www.SummerBridgeActivities.com

---

Page 81

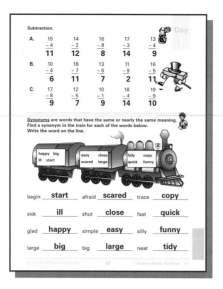

Subtraction.

A.	15	14	16	17	13
	− 4	− 2	− 8	− 3	− 4
	11	**12**	**8**	**14**	**9**
B.	10	18	13	11	16
	− 4	− 7	− 6	− 9	− 5
	6	**11**	**7**	**2**	**11**
C.	17	12	10	18	19
	− 8	− 5	− 1	− 4	− 9
	9	**7**	**9**	**14**	**10**

Synonyms are words that have the same or nearly the same meaning. Find a synonym in the train for each of the words below. Write the word on the line.

[train with words: happy, big, ill, start, easy, close, scared, large, tidy, copy, quick, funny]

begin **start**   afraid **scared**   trace **copy**

sick **ill**   shut **close**   fast **quick**

glad **happy**   simple **easy**   silly **funny**

large **big**   big **large**   neat **tidy**

Page 82

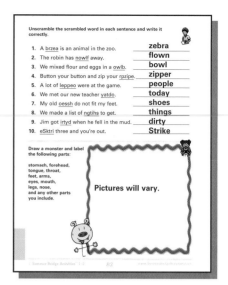

Unscramble the scrambled word in each sentence and write it correctly.

1. A *brzea* is an animal in the zoo. — **zebra**
2. The robin has *nowlf* away. — **flown**
3. We mixed flour and eggs in a *owlb*. — **bowl**
4. Button your button and zip your *rpzipe*. — **zipper**
5. A lot of *leppeo* were at the game. — **people**
6. We met our new teacher *yatdo*. — **today**
7. My old *oessh* do not fit my feet. — **shoes**
8. We made a list of *ngtihs* to get. — **things**
9. Jim got *irtyd* when he fell in the mud. — **dirty**
10. e*Sktri* three and you're out. — **Strike**

Draw a monster and label the following parts:

stomach, forehead, tongue, throat, feet, arms, eyes, mouth, legs, nose, and any other parts you include.

Pictures will vary.

Page 83

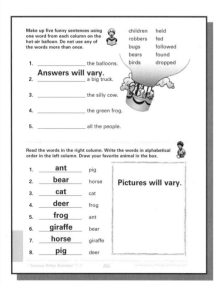

Addition.

3	6	9	5	4	3
5	4	2	1	3	3
+ 2	+ 3	+ 2	+ 2	+ 4	+ 4
10	**13**	**13**	**8**	**11**	**10**

4	7	1	6	2	8
5	2	8	1	3	2
+ 3	+ 1	+ 1	+ 4	+ 2	+ 3
12	**10**	**10**	**11**	**7**	**13**

7 + 3 + 1 = **11**   8 + 2 + 2 = **12**   3 + 5 + 1 = **9**

Read the sentences. Find a synonym in the Word Box for each underlined word. Write the new word on the lines. A synonym is a word that has the same or nearly the same meaning as another word.

automobile	small	glad	rush

The baby is very <u>tiny</u>. — **small**

The <u>car</u> ran out of gas. — **automobile**

Susan won, so she was very <u>happy</u>. — **glad**

My mother was in a big <u>hurry</u>. — **rush**

Page 84

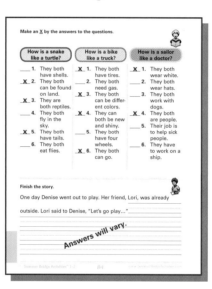

Make an X by the answers to the questions.

How is a snake like a turtle?
1. They both have shells.
X 2. They both can be found on land.
X 3. They are both reptiles.
4. They both fly in the sky.
X 5. They both have tails.
6. They both eat flies.

How is a bike like a truck?
X 1. They both have tires.
2. They both need gas.
X 3. They both can be different colors.
X 4. They can both be new and shiny.
5. They both have four wheels.
6. They both can go.

How is a sailor like a doctor?
X 1. They both wear white.
2. They both wear hats.
3. They both work with dogs.
X 4. They both are people.
5. Their job is to help sick people.
X 6. They have to work on a ship.

Finish the story.

One day Denise went out to play. Her friend, Lori, was already outside. Lori said to Denise, "Let's go play..."

Answers will vary.

Page 85

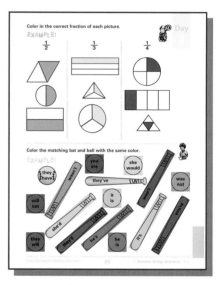

Color in the correct fraction of each picture.

EXAMPLE: $\frac{1}{2}$ $\frac{1}{3}$ $\frac{1}{4}$

Color the matching bat and ball with the same color.

EXAMPLE:

[bats and balls with: you are, they have, went, she would, was not, will not, it is, won't, she'd, they will, they'd, he is, it's, I've, you've]

Page 86

Make up five funny sentences using one word from each column on the hot-air balloon. Do not use any of the words more than once.

[balloon words: children, robbers, bugs, bears, birds, held, fed, followed, found, dropped]

1. _____ the balloons.
2. _____ a big truck.
3. _____ the silly cow.
4. _____ the green frog.
5. _____ all the people.

Answers will vary.

Read the words in the right column. Write the words in alphabetical order in the left column. Draw your favorite animal in the box.

1. **ant**	pig
2. **bear**	horse
3. **cat**	cat
4. **deer**	frog
5. **frog**	ant
6. **giraffe**	bear
7. **horse**	giraffe
8. **pig**	deer

Pictures will vary.

Page 87

Add or subtract.

11	18	3	10	17	13
+ 7	+ 1	+ 7	− 3	− 2	+ 6
18	**19**	**10**	**7**	**15**	**19**

33	64	5	2	12	14
+ 5	− 3	+ 3	+ 4	− 7	− 11
38	**61**	**8**	**6**	**5**	**3**

17 + 2 = **19**   11 − 3 = **8**   13 + 5 = **18**

Unscramble the words.

psto — **stop** or **pots** or **post** or **tops** or **spot**

sfat — **fast**

ltpae — **plate**

pste — **step** or **pets** or **pest**

gbrni — **bring**

rdnki — **drink**

enwt — **went** or **newt**

ithkn — **think**

oonn — **noon**

ppayh — **happy**

seay — **easy**

dbyo — **body**

stfri — **first**

yrc — **cry**

Page 88

Choose the best adjective from the Word List to complete each sentence.

Word List
funny
six
red
hard
oak
flying
furry

1. His kite got caught in that **oak** tree.
2. I can't believe you ate **six** hot dogs!
3. We laughed at the **funny** circus clowns.
4. Jackie got a **red** bike for Christmas.
5. My pillow is very **hard** and lumpy.
6. The rabbits all had soft and **furry** ears.

Circle the main idea of each picture.

1. The mother pays Rob and Tanner. / The mother is pretty.
2. The elves are wearing green. / **The elves are busy making shoes.**
3. The boys are wearing masks. / The boys are standing together.

Page 89

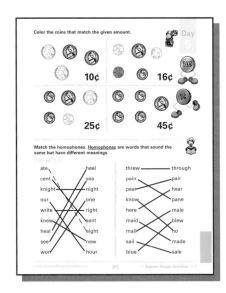

Color the coins that match the given amount.

10¢   16¢

25¢   45¢

Match the homophones. **Homophones** are words that sound the same but have different meanings.

EXAMPLE:

ate — heel
cent — sea
knight — night
our — one
write — right
knew — sent
heal — eight
see — new
won — hour

threw — through
pain — pair
pear — hear
know — pane
here — male
maid — blew
mail — no
sail — made
blue — sale

Page 90

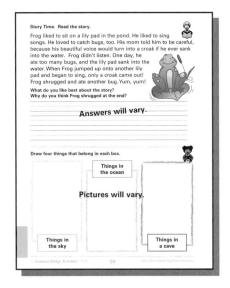

Story Time. Read the story.

Frog liked to sit on a lily pad in the pond. He liked to sing songs. He loved to catch bugs, too. His mom told him to be careful, because his beautiful voice would turn into a croak if he ever sank into the water. Frog didn't listen. One day, he ate too many bugs, and the lily pad sank into the water. When Frog jumped up onto another lily pad and began to sing, only a croak came out! Frog shrugged and ate another bug. Yum, yum!

What do you like best about the story?
Why do you think Frog shrugged at the end?

Answers will vary.

Draw four things that belong in each box.

Things in the ocean

Things in the sky

Things in a cave

Pictures will vary.

Page 91

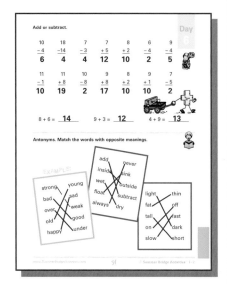

Add or subtract.

10 −4 = 6	18 −14 = 4	7 −3 = 4	7 +5 = 12	8 +2 = 10	9 −4 = 5
11 −1 = 10	11 +8 = 19	10 −8 = 2	9 +8 = 17	8 +2 = 10	9 +1 = 10	7 −5 = 2

8 + 6 = **14**   9 + 3 = **12**   4 + 9 = **13**

Antonyms. Match the words with opposite meanings.

EXAMPLE:

strong — young
bad — sad
over — weak
old — good
happy — under

add — never
inside — sink
wet — outside
float — subtract
always — dry

light — thin
fat — off
tall — fast
on — dark
slow — short

Page 92

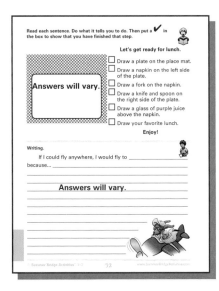

Read each sentence. Do what it tells you to do. Then put a ✔ in the box to show that you have finished that step.

Let's get ready for lunch.

Answers will vary.

☐ Draw a plate on the place mat.
☐ Draw a napkin on the left side of the plate.
☐ Draw a fork on the napkin.
☐ Draw a knife and spoon on the right side of the plate.
☐ Draw a glass of purple juice above the napkin.
☐ Draw your favorite lunch.

Enjoy!

Writing.

If I could fly anywhere, I would fly to _____ because...

Answers will vary.

Page 93

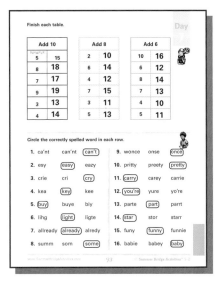

Finish each table.

Add 10	
5	15
8	18
7	17
9	19
3	13
4	14

Add 8	
2	10
6	14
4	12
7	15
3	11
5	13

Add 6	
10	16
6	12
8	14
7	13
4	10
5	11

Circle the correctly spelled word in each row.

1. ca'nt   can'nt   **can't**
2. esy   **easy**   eazy
3. crie   cri   **cry**
4. kea   **key**   kee
5. **buy**   buye   biy
6. lihg   **light**   ligte
7. allready   **already**   alredy
8. summ   som   **some**
9. wonce   onse   **once**
10. pritty   preety   **pretty**
11. **carry**   carey   carrie
12. **you're**   yure   yo're
13. parte   **part**   parrt
14. **star**   stor   starr
15. funy   **funny**   funnie
16. babie   babey   **baby**

Page 94

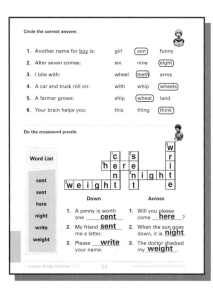

Circle the correct answer.

1. Another name for <u>boy</u> is: girl   **son**   funny
2. After seven comes: six   nine   **eight**
3. I bite with: wheel   **teeth**   arms
4. A car and truck roll on: with   whip   **wheels**
5. A farmer grows: ship   **wheat**   land
6. Your brain helps you: this   thing   **think**

Do the crossword puzzle.

Word List
cent
sent
here
night
write
weight

(crossword: write, here, night, weight)

Down
1. A penny is worth one **cent**
2. My friend **sent** me a letter.
3. Please **write** your name.

Across
1. Will you please come **here** ?
2. When the sun goes down, it is **night**.
3. The doctor checked my **weight**.

Page 95

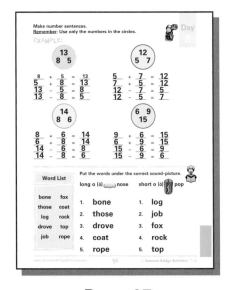

Make number sentences.
<u>Remember:</u> Use only the numbers in the circles.

EXAMPLE:

13
8 5

8 + 5 = 13
5 + 8 = 13
13 − 5 = 8
13 − 8 = 5

12
5 7

5 + 7 = 12
7 + 5 = 12
12 − 7 = 5
12 − 5 = 7

14
8 6

8 + 6 = 14
6 + 8 = 14
14 − 6 = 8
14 − 8 = 6

6 9
15

6 + 9 = 15
9 + 6 = 15
15 − 9 = 6
15 − 6 = 9

Word List
bone   fox
those   coat
log   rock
drove   top
job   rope

Put the words under the correct sound-picture.

long o (ō) nose
1. bone
2. those
3. drove
4. coat
5. rope

short o (ŏ) pop
1. log
2. job
3. fox
4. rock
5. top

Page 96

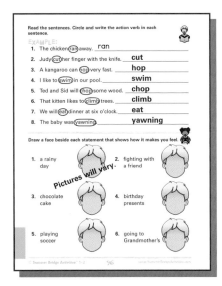

Read the sentences. Circle and write the action verb in each sentence.

EXAMPLE:
1. The chicken (ran) away.   **ran**
2. Judy (cut) her finger with the knife.   **cut**
3. A kangaroo can (hop) very fast.   **hop**
4. I like to (swim) in our pool.   **swim**
5. Ted and Sid will (chop) some wood.   **chop**
6. That kitten likes to (climb) trees.   **climb**
7. We will (eat) dinner at six o'clock.   **eat**
8. The baby was (yawning).   **yawning**

Draw a face beside each statement that shows how it makes you feel.

1. a rainy day
2. fighting with a friend
3. chocolate cake
4. birthday presents
5. playing soccer
6. going to Grandmother's

Pictures will vary.

Page 97

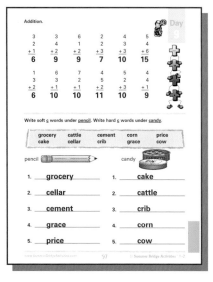

Addition.

3 2 +1 = 6	3 4 +2 = 9	6 2 +1 = 9	2 2 +3 = 7	4 3 +3 = 10	5 4 +6 = 15
1 3 +2 = 6	6 3 +1 = 10	7 2 +1 = 10	4 5 +2 = 11	3 6 +1 = 10	3 5 +1 = 9

Write soft c words under <u>pencil</u>. Write hard <u>c</u> words under <u>candy</u>.

grocery   cattle   cement   corn   price
cake   cellar   crib   grace   cow

pencil
1. **grocery**
2. **cellar**
3. **cement**
4. **grace**
5. **price**

candy
1. **cake**
2. **cattle**
3. **crib**
4. **corn**
5. **cow**

Page 98

Unscramble the sentences. Write the words in the correct order.

1. sun shine will today The.

The sun will shine today.

2. mile today I a walked.

I walked a mile today.

3. house We painted our.

We painted our house.

4. Mother knit will I something for.

I will knit something for Mother.

Write a letter. Ask someone to a silly picnic.

Start your letter with "Dear _____."
End your letter with "Yours truly, _____."

Answers will vary.

Page 99

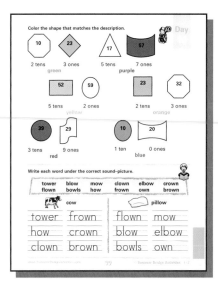

Color the shape that matches the description.

10	23	17	57
2 tens	3 ones	5 tens	7 ones
green		purple	

52	59	23	32
5 tens	2 ones	2 tens	3 ones
yellow		orange	

39	29	10	20
3 tens	9 ones	1 ten	0 ones
red		blue	

Write each word under the correct sound-picture.

tower blow mow clown elbow crown
flown bowls how frown own brown

cow
tower	frown
how	crown
clown	brown

pillow
flown	mow
blow	elbow
bowls	own

Page 100

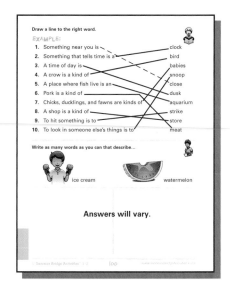

Draw a line to the right word.

EXAMPLE:

1. Something near you is
2. Something that tells time is a
3. A time of day is
4. A crow is a kind of
5. A place where fish live is an
6. Pork is a kind of
7. Chicks, ducklings, and fawns are kinds of
8. A shop is a kind of
9. To hit something is to
10. To look in someone else's things is to

clock
bird
babies
snoop
close
dusk
aquarium
strike
store
meat

Write as many words as you can that describe...

ice cream   watermelon

Answers will vary.

Page 101

Subtract.

57	68	96	57	38	59
− 32	− 44	− 92	− 43	− 3	− 45
25	24	4	14	35	14

83	75	48	95	68	39	89
− 62	− 20	− 4	− 31	− 26	− 10	− 53
21	55	44	64	42	29	36

19	24	52	63	76	88	90
− 3	− 11	− 31	− 41	− 22	− 44	− 30
16	13	21	22	54	44	60

Write in the name of each picture and color.

so c k   gr a ss   f i sh

sh i r t   s t ove   gat e

Page 102

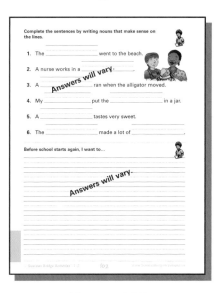

Complete the sentences by writing nouns that make sense on the lines.

1. The _____ went to the beach.

2. A nurse works in a _____.

3. A _____ ran when the alligator moved.

4. My _____ put the _____ in a jar.

5. A _____ tastes very sweet.

6. The _____ made a lot of _____.

Answers will vary.

Before school starts again, I want to...

Answers will vary.

Page 103

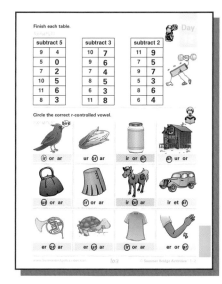

Finish each table.

subtract 5		subtract 3		subtract 2	
9	4	10	7	11	9
5	0	9	6	7	5
7	2	7	4	9	7
10	5	8	5	8	6
11	6	8	5	8	6
8	3	11	8	6	4

Circle the correct r-controlled vowel.

ir or ar   ur or ar   ir or ir   an ur or

ur or ar   ir or ar   ir or ar   ir et ar

er or ar   er ur ar   ir or ar   er or ar

Page 104

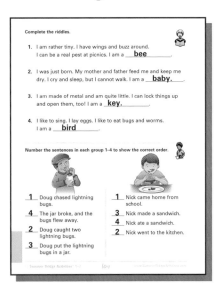

Complete the riddles.

1. I am rather tiny. I have wings and buzz around. I can be a real pest at picnics. I am a **bee**.

2. I was just born. My mother and father feed me and keep me dry. I cry and sleep, but I cannot walk. I am a **baby.**

3. I am made of metal and am quite little. I can lock things up and open them, too! I am a **key.**

4. I like to sing. I lay eggs. I like to eat bugs and worms. I am a **bird**

Number the sentences in each group 1–4 to show the correct order.

1 Doug chased lightning bugs.
4 The jar broke, and the bugs flew away.
2 Doug caught two lightning bugs.
3 Doug put the lightning bugs in a jar.

1 Nick came home from school.
3 Nick made a sandwich.
4 Nick ate a sandwich.
2 Nick went to the kitchen.

Page 105

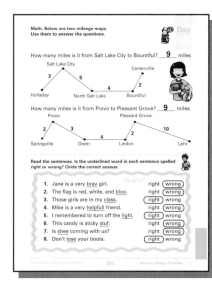

Math. Below are two mileage maps. Use them to answer the questions.

How many miles is it from Salt Lake City to Bountiful? **9** miles

How many miles is it from Provo to Pleasant Grove? **9** miles

Read the sentences. Is the underlined word in each sentence spelled right or wrong? Circle the correct answer.

1. Jane is a very brav girl. right (wrong)
2. The flag is red, white, and bloo. right (wrong)
3. Those girls are in my class. (right) wrong
4. Mike is a very helpfull friend. right (wrong)
5. I remembered to turn off the light. (right) wrong
6. This candy is sticky stuf. right (wrong)
7. Is shee coming with us? right (wrong)
8. Don't lose your boots. (right) wrong

Page 106

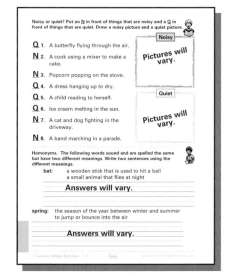

Noisy or quiet? Put an N in front of things that are noisy and a Q in front of things that are quiet. Draw a noisy picture and a quiet picture.

Q 1. A butterfly flying through the air.
N 2. A cook using a mixer to make a cake.
N 3. Popcorn popping on the stove.
Q 4. A dress hanging up to dry.
Q 5. A child reading to herself.
Q 6. Ice cream melting in the sun.
N 7. A cat and dog fighting in the driveway.
N 8. A band marching in a parade.

Noisy — Pictures will vary.
Quiet — Pictures will vary.

Homonyms. The following words sound and are spelled the same but have two different meanings. Write two sentences using the different meanings.

bat: a wooden stick that is used to hit a ball
        a small animal that flies at night

Answers will vary.

spring: the season of the year between winter and summer
           to jump or bounce into the air

Answers will vary.

Page 107

Add or subtract.

24 + 12 **36**	16 − 0 **16**	28 − 14 **14**	37 − 26 **11**	42 + 27 **69**	12 + 11 **23**
87¢ − 16¢ **71¢**	79¢ − 54¢ **25¢**	3 + 13 **16**	15¢ + 24¢ **39¢**	97 − 64 **33**	40 + 40 **80**
12 40 + 62 **114**	18 20 + 11 **49**	41 6 + 32 **79**	66 22 + 11 **99**	13 22 + 24 **59**	30 12 + 10 **52**

Circle either g or j below each word to show which sound the g makes.

giant g **j** — girl **g** j — gentle g **j** — game **g** j — gym g **j**

cage g **j** — angel g **j** — giraffe g **j** — goat **g** j — again **g** j — frog **g** j

gate g **j** — change g **j** — badger **g** j

golf **g** j — dragon g **j** — go **g** j

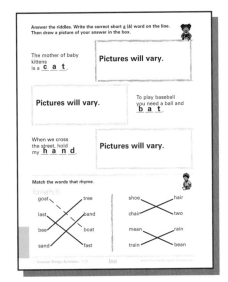

Page 108

Answer the riddles. Write the correct short g (ā) word on the line. Then draw a picture of your answer in the box.

The mother of baby kittens is a **c a t** .

Pictures will vary.

Pictures will vary.

To play baseball you need a ball and **b a t** .

When we cross the street, hold my **h a n d** .

Pictures will vary.

Match the words that rhyme.

EXAMPLE:
goat — tree
last — band
bee — boat
sand — fast

shoe — hair
chair — two
mean — rain
train — bean

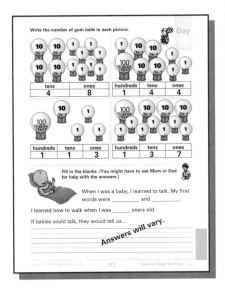

Page 109

Write the number of gum balls in each picture.

tens	ones
4	8

hundreds	tens	ones
1	4	4

hundreds	tens	ones
1	1	3

hundreds	tens	ones
1	3	7

Fill in the blanks. (You might have to ask Mom or Dad for help with the answers.)

When I was a baby, I learned to talk. My first words were _____ and _____.

I learned how to walk when I was _____ years old.

If babies could talk, they would tell us...

Answers will vary.

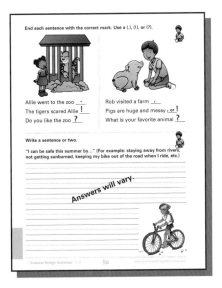

Page 110

End each sentence with the correct mark. Use a (.), (!), or (?).

Allie went to the zoo **.**
The tigers scared Allie **!**
Do you like the zoo **?**

Rob visited a farm **.**
Pigs are huge and messy **. or !**
What is your favorite animal **?**

Write a sentence or two.

"I can be safe this summer by..." (For example: staying away from rivers, not getting sunburned, keeping my bike out of the road when I ride, etc.)

Answers will vary.

Up until now, **Summer Bridge Activities**™ has been all about your mind...

But the other parts of you—who you are, how you act, and how you feel—are important too. These pages are all about helping build a better you this summer.

Keeping your body strong and healthy helps you live better, learn better, and feel better. To keep your body healthy, you need to do things like eat right, get enough sleep, and exercise. The Physical Fitness pages of Building Better Bodies will teach you about good eating habits and the importance of proper exercise. You can even train for a Presidential Fitness Award over the summer.

The Character pages are all about building a better you on the inside. They've got fun activities for you and your family to do together. The activities will help you develop important values and habits you'll need as you grow up.

After a summer of Building Better Bodies and Behavior and **Summer Bridge Activities**™, there may be a whole new you ready for school in the fall!

For Parents: Introduction to Character Education

Character education is simply giving your child clear messages about the values you and your family consider important. Many studies have shown that a basic core of values is universal. You will find certain values reflected in the laws of every country and incorporated in the teachings of religious, ethical, and other belief systems throughout the world.

The character activities included here are designed to span the entire summer. Each week your child will be introduced to a new value, with a quote and two activities that illustrate it. Research has shown that character education is most effective when parents reinforce the values in their child's daily routine; therefore, we encourage parents to be involved as their child completes the lessons.

Here are some suggestions on how to maximize these lessons.
- Read through the lesson yourself. Then set aside a block of time for you and your child to discuss the value.
- Plan a block of time to work on the suggested activities.
- Discuss the meaning of the quote with your child. Ask, "What do you think the quote means?" Have your child ask other members of the family the same question. If possible, include grandparents, aunts, uncles, and cousins.
- Use the quote as often as you can during the week. You'll be pleasantly surprised to learn that both you and your child will have it memorized by the end of the week.
- For extra motivation, you can set a reward for completing each week's activities.
- Point out to your child other people who are actively displaying a value. Example: "See how John is helping Mrs. Olsen by raking her leaves."
- Be sure to praise your child each time he or she practices a value: "Mary, it was very courteous of you to wait until I finished speaking."
- Find time in your day to talk about values. Turn off the radio in the car and chat with your children; take a walk in the evening as a family; read a story about the weekly value at bedtime; or give a back rub while you talk about what makes your child happy or sad.
- Finally, model the values you want your child to acquire. Remember, children will do as you do, not as you say.

Name _____ Date _____

How I Measure Up!

You will be filling in this page twice—once now and once at the end of the summer to see how you have grown. Have an adult help you measure yourself to fill in the blanks below.

around the neck ___/___

smile ___/___

neck to belly button ___/___

around the wrist ___/___

around the neck ___/___

shoulder to elbow ___/___

elbow to wrist ___/___

around the waist ___/___

waist to ankle ___/___

around the wrist ___/___

around the waist ___/___

length of longest finger ___/___

waist to ankle ___/___

around the knee ___/___

around the ankle ___/___

around the ankle ___/___

foot length ___/___

around the knee ___/___

length of longest finger ___/___

smile ___/___

neck to belly button ___/___

shoulder to elbow ___/___

elbow to wrist ___/___

foot length ___/___

Building Better Bodies and Behavior

128

© Summer Bridge Activities™

Nutrition

The food you eat helps your body grow. It gives you energy to work and play. Some foods give you protein or fats. Other foods provide vitamins, minerals, or carbohydrates. These are all things your body needs. Eating a variety of good foods each day will help you stay healthy. How much and what foods you need depends on many things, including whether you're a girl or boy, how active you are, and how old you are. To figure out the right amount of food for you, go to http://www.mypyramid.gov/mypyramid/index.aspx and use the Pyramid Plan Calculator. In the meantime, here are some general guidelines.

Your body needs nutrients from each food group every day.

Grains	Vegetables	Fruits	Oils	Milk	Meat & Beans
4 to 5 ounce equivalents each day (an ounce might be a slice of bread, a packet of oatmeal, or a bowl of cereal)	1 1/2 cups each day	1 to 1 1/2 cups each day		1 to 2 cups of milk (or other calcium-rich food) each day	3 to 5 ounce equivalents each day

Put a ▢ around the four foods from the Grains Group.

Put a △ around the two foods from the Meat and Beans Group.

Put a ◇ around the three foods from the Milk Group.

Put a ○ around the two foods from the Fruits Group.

Put a ▭ around the four foods from the Vegetables Group.

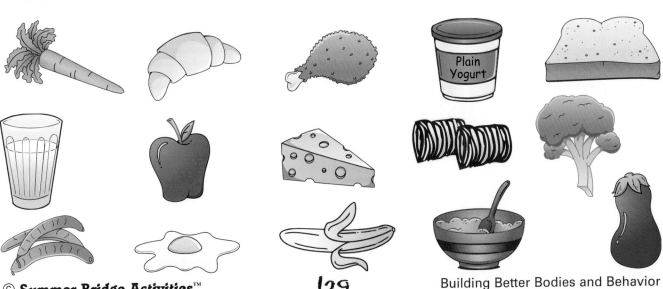

129

Building Better Bodies and Behavior

Foods I Need Each Day

Plan out three balanced meals for one day. Arrange your meals so that by the end of the day, you will have had all the recommended amounts of food from each food group listed on the food pyramid.

Grains—4 to 5 oz. equivalents
(an ounce might be a slice of bread, a packet of oatmeal, or a bowl of cereal)

Vegetables—1 1/2 cups

Fruits—1 to 1 1/2 cups

Milk—1 to 2 cups

Meat and Beans—3 to 4 oz. equivalents
(a hamburger, half a chicken breast, or a can of tuna would be 3–4 ounces)

Draw or cut and paste pictures of the types of food you need each day.

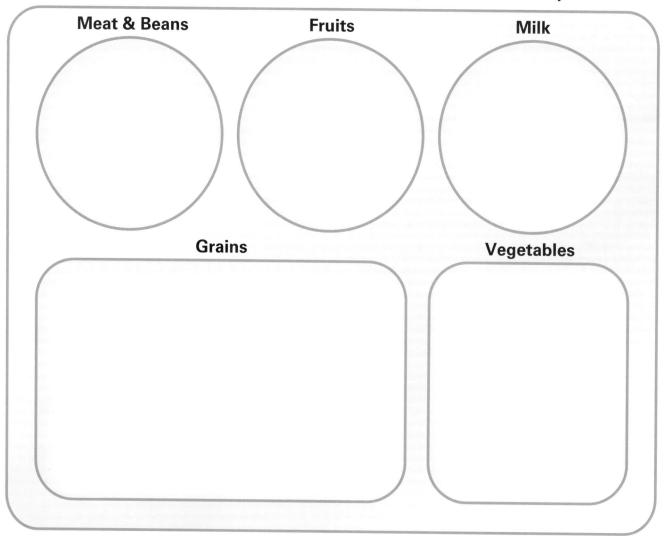

Meat & Beans   Fruits   Milk

Grains   Vegetables

Meal Tracker

Use these charts to record the amount of food you eat from each food group for one or two weeks. Have another family member keep track, too, and compare.

	Grains	Milk	Meat & Beans	Fruits	Vegetables	Oils
Monday						
Tuesday						
Wednesday						
Thursday						
Friday						
Saturday						
Sunday						

	Grains	Milk	Meat & Beans	Fruits	Vegetables	Oils
Monday						
Tuesday						
Wednesday						
Thursday						
Friday						
Saturday						
Sunday						

Get Moving!

Did you know that getting no exercise can be almost as bad for you as smoking? So get moving this summer!

Summer is the perfect time to get out and get in shape. Your fitness program should include three parts:

- Get 30 minutes of aerobic exercise per day, three to five days a week.

- Exercise your muscles to improve strength and flexibility.

- Make it FUN! Do things that you like to do. Include your friends and family.

Couch Potato Quiz

1. Name three things you do each day that get you moving.

2. Name three things you do a few times a week that are good exercise.

3. How many hours do you spend each week playing outside or exercising?

4. How much TV do you watch each day?

5. How much time do you spend playing computer or video games?

If the time you spend on activities 4 and 5 adds up to more than you spend on 1–3, you could be headed for a spud's life!

**You can find information on fitness at
www.fitness.gov or www.kidshealth.org**

Building Better Bodies and Behavior

132

© Summer Bridge Activities™

Activity Pyramid

The Activity Pyramid works like the Food Pyramid. You can use the Activity Pyramid to help plan your summer exercise program. Fill in the blanks below.

List 1 thing that isn't good exercise that you could do less of this summer.

1._____

Cut Down On
TV time
video or computer games
sitting for more than
30 minutes at a time

List 3 fun activities you enjoy that get you moving and are good exercise.

1._____
2._____
3._____

List 3 exercises you could do to build strength and flexibility this summer.

1._____
2._____
3._____

2–3 Times a Week

Work & Play
bowling
swinging
fishing
jump rope
yard work

Strength & Stretching
dancing
martial arts
gymnastics
push-ups/pull-ups

List 3 activities you would like to do for aerobic exercise this summer.

1._____
2._____
3._____

List 2 sports you would like to participate in this summer.

1._____
2._____

3–5 Times a Week
at least 30 minutes

Aerobic Exercise
walking   skating
running   bicycling
             swimming

Sports/Recreation
soccer   relay races
basketball   tennis
volleyball   baseball

Every Day

walk
play outside
take the stairs
bathe your pet

help with chores:
sweeping
washing dishes
picking up
clothes and toys

Adapted from the President's Council on Fitness and Sports

List 5 everyday things you can do to get moving more often.

1._____
2._____
3._____
4._____
5._____

Fitness Fundamentals

Basic physical fitness includes several things:

Cardiovascular Endurance. Your cardiovascular system includes your heart and blood vessels. You need a strong heart to pump your blood which delivers oxygen and nutrients to your body.

Muscular Strength. This is how strong your muscles are.

Muscular Endurance. Endurance has to do with how long you can use your muscles before they get tired.

Flexibility. This is your ability to move your joints and to use your muscles through their full range of motion.

Body Composition. Your body is made up of lean mass and fat mass.

Lean mass includes the water, muscles, tissues, and organs in your body.

Fat mass includes the fat your body stores for energy. Exercise helps you burn body fat and maintain good body composition.

The goal of a summer fitness program is to improve in all the areas of physical fitness.

You build cardiovascular endurance through **aerobic** exercise. For **aerobic** exercise, you need to work large muscle groups at a steady pace. This increases your heart rate and breathing. You can jog, walk, hike, swim, dance, do aerobics, ride a bike, go rowing, climb stairs, rollerblade, play golf, backpack…

You should get at least 30 minutes of aerobic exercise per day, three to five days a week.

You build muscular strength and endurance with exercises that work your muscles, like sit-ups, push-ups, pull-ups, and weight lifting.

You can increase flexibility through stretching exercises. These are good for warm-ups, too.

Draw a stick person. Give your person a heart (for aerobic exercise), muscles in the arms (for strength and endurance), and bent knees (for flexibility).

Your Summer Fitness Program

Start your summer fitness program by choosing at least one aerobic activity from your Activity Pyramid. You can choose more than one for variety.

_____   _____   _____

Do this activity three to five times each week. Keep it up for at least 30 minutes each time.
(Exercise hard enough to increase your heart rate and your breathing. Don't exercise so hard that you get dizzy or can't catch your breath.)

Use this chart to plan when you will exercise, or use it as a record when you exercise.

DATE	ACTIVITY	TIME

DATE	ACTIVITY	TIME

Plan a reward for meeting your exercise goals for two weeks.
(You can make copies of this chart to track your fitness all summer long.)

Start Slow!

Remember to start out slow. Exercise is about getting stronger. It's not about being superman—or superwoman—right off the bat.

Are You Up to the Challenge?

The Presidential Physical Fitness Award Program was designed to help kids get into shape and have fun. To earn the award, you take five fitness tests. These are usually given by teachers at school, but you can train for them this summer. Make a chart to track your progress. Keep working all summer to see if you can improve your score.

Remember: Start Slow!

1. Curl-ups. Lie on the floor with your knees bent and your feet about 12 inches from your buttocks. Cross your arms over your chest. Raise your trunk up and touch your elbows to your thighs. Do as many as you can in one minute.

 2. Shuttle Run. Draw a starting line. Put two blocks 30 feet away. Run the 30 feet, pick up a block, and bring it back to the starting line. Then run and bring back the second block. Record your fastest time.

3. V-sit Reach. Sit on the floor with your legs straight and your feet 8 to 12 inches apart. Put a ruler between your feet, pointing past your toes. Have a partner hold your legs straight, and keep your toes pointed up. Link your thumbs together and reach forward, palms down, as far as you can along the ruler.

 4. One-Mile Walk/Run. On a track or some safe area, run one mile. You can walk as often as you need to. Finish as fast as possible. (Ages six to seven may want to run a quarter mile; ages eight to nine, half a mile.)

5. Pull-ups. Grip a bar with an overhand grip (the backs of your hands toward your face). Have someone lift you up if you need help. Hang with your arms and legs straight. Pull your body up until your chin is over the bar; then let yourself back down. Do as many as you can.

Respect

Respect is showing good manners toward all people, not just those you know or who are like you. Respect is treating everyone, no matter what religion, race, or culture, male or female, rich or poor, in a way that you would want to be treated. The easiest way to do this is to decide to **never** take part in activities and to **never** use words that make fun of people because they are different from you or your friends.

Treat others as you would like to be treated.

~ The Golden Rule

Color the picture below.

Activity

This week go to the library and check out *Bein' with You This Way* by W. Nikola-Lisa (1995). This book is a fun rap about things that make us different and things that make us the same. Read it with your parents!

Gratitude

Gratitude is when you thank people for the good things they have given you or done for you. Thinking about people and events in your life that make you feel grateful (thankful) will help you become a happier person.

There are over 465 different ways of saying thank you. Here are a few:

Danke   *Toda*   *Merci*   Gracias   **Nandri**
Spasibo   Arigato   **Gadda ge**   Paldies   Hvala

Make a list of ten things you are grateful for.

1. _____   6. _____

2. _____   7. _____

3. _____   8. _____

4. _____   9. _____

5. _____   10. _____

A Recipe for Saying Thanks

1. Make a colorful card.

2. On the inside, write a thank-you note to someone who has done something nice for you.

3. Address an envelope to that person.

4. Pick out a cool stamp.

5. Drop your note in the nearest mailbox.

> **Saying thank you creates love.**
> ~ Daphne Rose Kingma

Manners

If you were the only person in the world, you wouldn't have to have **good manners** or be **courteous**. However, there are over six billion people on our planet, and good manners help us all get along with each other.

Children with good manners are usually well liked by other children and are certainly liked by adults. Here are some simple rules for good manners:

• When you ask for something, say, "Please."
• When someone gives you something, say, "Thank you."
• When someone says, "Thank you," say, "You're welcome."
• If you walk in front of someone or bump into a person, say, "Excuse me."
• When someone else is talking, wait before speaking.
• Share and take turns.

> No kindness, no matter how small, is ever wasted. ~ **Aesop's Fables**

See How I'm Nice

(sung to "Three Blind Mice")

See how I'm nice,
see how I'm nice.
Thanks, thanks, thanks.
Please, please, please.
I cover my nose whenever I sneeze.
I sit on my chair, not on my knees.
I always say "thank you" when
I'm passed some peas.
Thanks, thanks, thanks.
Please, please, please.

I've Got Manners

Make a colorful poster to display on your bedroom door or on the refrigerator. List five ways you are going to practice your manners. Be creative and decorate with watercolors, poster paints, pictures cut from magazines, clip art, or geometric shapes.

Instead of making a poster, you could make a mobile to hang from your ceiling that shows five different manners to practice.

Choices

A **choice** is when you get to pick between two or more things. Often, one choice is better for you than another. Spend time thinking about which choice would be best for you before you make a decision.

Let's Practice. Pick which you think is the best choice:

1. What might be best for you to eat?
   a. an apple   b. a candy bar   c. potato chips

2. What is a good time to go to bed on a school night?
   a. midnight   b. 8:00 P.M.   c. noon

3. If a friend pushes you, you should
   a. cry.   b. hit him/her.   c. tell your friend, in a nice voice, that you don't like being pushed.

Activity

Get a copy of *The Tale of Peter Rabbit* by Beatrix Potter. Read it out loud with an adult. Talk about the choices Peter made during the story. Are there other choices that would have been better?

Color the picture below.

Friendship

Friends come in all sizes, shapes, and ages: brothers, sisters, parents, neighbors, good teachers, and school and sports friends.

There is a saying, "To have a friend you need to be a friend." Can you think of a day when someone might have tried to get you to say or do unkind things to someone else? Sometimes it takes courage to be a real friend. Did you have the courage to say no?

A Recipe for Friendship

1 cup of always listening to ideas and stories
2 pounds of never talking behind a friend's back
1 pound of no mean teasing
2 cups of always helping a friend who needs help

Take these ingredients and mix completely together. Add laughter, kindness, hugs, and even tears. Bake for as long as it takes to make your friendship good and strong.

It's so much more friendly with two.

~ A. A. Milne
(creator of Winnie the Pooh)

Family Night at the Movies

Rent *Toy Story* or *Toy Story II*. Each movie is a simple, yet powerful, tale about true friendship. Fix a big bowl of popcorn to share with your family during the show.

International Friendship Day

The first Sunday in August is International Friendship Day. This is a perfect day to remember all your friends and how they have helped you during your friendship. Give your friends a call or send them an email or snail-mail card.

Confidence

People are **confident** or have **confidence** when they feel like they can succeed at a certain task. To feel confident about doing something, most people need to practice a task over and over.

Reading, pitching a baseball, writing in cursive, playing the flute, even mopping a floor are all examples of tasks that need to be practiced before people feel confident they can succeed.

What are five things you feel confident doing?

What is one thing you want to feel more confident doing?

Make a plan for how and when you will practice until you feel confident.

- -

You Crack Me Up!

Materials needed:
1 dozen eggs
a mixing bowl

Cracking eggs without breaking the yolk or getting egg whites all over your hands takes practice.

1. Watch an adult break an egg into the bowl. How did they hold their hands? How did they pull the egg apart?

2. Now you try. Did you do a perfect job the first time? Keep trying until you begin to feel confident about cracking eggs.

3. Use the eggs immediately to make a cheese omelet or custard pie. Refrigerate any unused eggs for up to three days.

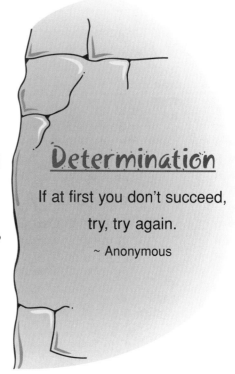

Determination

If at first you don't succeed,

try, try again.

~ Anonymous

Responsibility

You show **responsibility** by doing what you agree or promise to do. It might be a task, such as a homework assignment, or a chore, such as feeding your fish.

When you are young, your parents and teachers will give you simple tasks like putting away toys or brushing your teeth without being asked. As you get older, you will be given more responsibility. You might be trusted to come home from a friend's house at a certain time or drive to the store for groceries.

It takes a lot of practice to grow up to be a responsible person. The easiest way to practice is by keeping your promises and doing what you know is right.

A parent is responsible for different things than a child or a teenager. Write three activities you are responsible for every day. Then write three things a parent is responsible for every day.

If you want your eggs hatched, sit on them yourself. ~ Haitian Proverb

Activity

Materials needed:
21 pennies or counters such as beans, rocks, or marbles
2 small containers labeled #1 and #2

Decide on a reward for successfully completing this activity.
Put all the counters in container #1.
Review the three activities you are responsible for every day.
Each night before you go to bed, put one counter for each completed activity into container #2. At the end of seven days count all the counters in container #2.
If you have 16 or more counters in container #2, you are on your way to becoming very responsible. Collect your reward.

My reward is_____.

Service/Helping

Service is **helping** another person or group of people without asking for any kind of reward or payment. These are some good things that happen when you do service:

1. You feel closer to the people in your community (neighborhood).
2. You feel pride in yourself when you see that you can help other people in need.
3. Your family feels proud of you.
4. You will make new friends as you help others.

An old saying goes, "Charity begins at home." This means that you don't have to do big, important-sounding things to help people. You can start in your own home and neighborhood.

Activity

Each day this week, do one act of service around your house. Don't ask for or take any kind of payment or reward. Be creative! Possible acts of service are

1. Carry in the groceries, do the dishes, or fold the laundry.
2. Read aloud to a younger brother or sister.
3. Make breakfast or pack lunches.
4. Recycle newspapers and cans.
5. Clean the refrigerator or your room.

At the end of the week, think of a project to do with your family that will help your community. You could play musical instruments or sing at a nursing home, set up a lemonade stand and give the money you make to the Special Olympics, offer to play board games with children in the hospital, or pick some flowers and take them to a neighbor. The list goes on and on.

Actions speak louder than words.
~ Anonymous

Color the picture below.

Honesty and Trust

Being an **honest** person means you don't steal, cheat, or tell lies. **Trust** is when you believe someone will be honest. If you are dishonest, or not truthful, people will not trust you.

You want to tell the truth because it is important to have your family and friends trust you. However, it takes courage to tell the truth, especially if you don't want people to get mad at you or be disappointed in the way you behaved.

How would your parents feel if you lied to them? People almost always find out about lies, and most parents will be more angry about a lie than if you had told them the truth in the first place.

When family or friends ask about something, remember that honesty is telling the truth. Honesty is telling what really happened. Honesty is keeping your promises. *Be proud of being an honest person.*

Color the picture.

Parent note: Help your child by pointing out times he or she acted honestly.

Count to Ten

Tape ten pieces of colored paper to your refrigerator. For one week, each time you tell the truth or keep a promise, take one piece of paper down and put it in the recycling bin. If all ten pieces of paper are gone by the end of the week, collect your reward.

Most Improved

Honesty is the first chapter in the book of wisdom.
~Thomas Jefferson

My reward is_____.

Happiness

Happiness is a feeling that comes when you enjoy your life. Different things make different people happy. Some people feel happy when they are playing soccer. Other people feel happy when they are playing the cello. It is important to understand what makes you happy so you can include some of these things in your daily plan.

These are some actions that show you are happy: laughing, giggling, skipping, smiling, and hugging.

Make a list of five activities that make you feel happy.

1.
2.
3.
4.
5.

Bonus!

List two things you could do to make someone else happy.

1._____

2._____

Activity

Write down a plan to do one activity each day this week that makes you happy.

Try simple things—listen to your favorite song, play with a friend, bake muffins, shoot hoops, etc.

Be sure to thank everyone who helps you, and don't forget to laugh!

Happy Thought

The world is so full

of a number of things,

I'm sure we should

all be happy as kings.

~Robert Louis Stevenson

Notes

_____

_____

_____

_____

_____

_____

_____

_____

_____

_____

_____

_____

_____

_____

_____

_____

_____

_____

5 <u>Five things I'm thankful for:</u>

1. _____

2. _____

3. _____

4. _____

5. _____

Notes

_____

_____

_____

_____

_____

_____

_____

_____

_____

_____

_____

_____

_____

_____

_____

_____

_____

_____

5 Five things I'm thankful for:

1. _____

2. _____

3. _____

4. _____

5. _____

Activities for Addition and Subtraction Cards

Use the flashcards to practice addition and subtraction facts from 0-10. Make piles of facts you know and facts you need help on. Review the pile of cards you need help on until you are an addition/subtraction expert!

Each card shows an addition or subtraction fact on each side. On the opposite side of the card, the answer to the equation is shown in the lower left-hand corner. Addition facts are colored magenta and the subtraction facts are shown in green.

Enrichment Activities for Sound Cards

Assess what your child knows and understands, then use only those activities your child needs.

Parents, when you are working with the letter sounds and the sound blending process, you may exaggerate the letter sounds, but be careful you don't distort them.

When working with the letter sounds, sound blending, and word recognition, you need to help your child learn that these sound words usually work this way but there are words that "do not follow the rules."

Consonants

1. Consonant recognition—Start with the consonant sound cards first. Explain that the letters of the alphabet have letter names and letter sounds. Identify the consonant letters and tell your child that these are called consonants because they usually have only one sound.

2. Take just a few (1 to 3) sound cards at a time. Identify the letter name on the front and the sound picture on the back. Exaggerate the beginning sound. Now, say two words to help your child choose the word that starts with the same beginning sound as the sound card you are working with. When he/she becomes familiar and successful with this process, you can increase the number of sound cards you are working with.

3. Give your child 3 to 5 sound cards. Say a word or name an object and have him/her hold up the sound card beginning with the same sound.

4. Play the slap game. Say the sounds and/or words and have your child identify the sound card by slapping it.

5. As the child gets better at this, have him/her say a sound and/or word and see if he/she can beat you at the slap game mentioned in the activity above.

6. Have your child label his/her toys by their beginning sound. Give him/her small pieces of paper. Have him/her write down the letter or sound he/she thinks it begins with and place the paper by the toy or on top of it. See if the child can find 2 or more toys that begin with the same sound.

7. Activities 2 through 6 can be used to identify and understand ending sounds (the sound the objects end with).

Vowels

1. Explain to your child that vowels have more than one sound. Identify and teach the short vowel sounds before proceeding with the long vowel sounds.

2. Start with the short "a" vowel sound card. Show your child the apple on the back. Say the word "apple," then say it again, exaggerating the "a" sound. Have your child repeat the procedure,

then say, "Apple begins with the short 'a' sound."

3. Say 2 or more words and help your child identify those words that begin with the short "a" sound. (Example: ax, astronaut, octopus.)

4. Tell your child there are a lot of words that have the short "a" sound in them, such as "pat," "can," and "man." Next, say two or more words, varying short vowel and long vowel sounds. Then help your child identify which words have the short "a" sound in them.

5. Help your child learn to sound out or sound blend very simple short "a" words (example: can, fat, nap) by writing them on paper, chalkboard, magic slate, cards, etc.

6. Use activities for the other short vowel sounds of e, i, o, and u.

7. Use the consonant sound cards with the short vowel sound cards to put together simple words.

EXAMPLE:

Using the first letter sound of picture side of card.

Using the letters on the other side of card to make the word "man."

8. Follow the same procedure as #7, only this time change just the beginning sound or letter card to make new words (rhyming words). (Example: man, fan, ran, can, etc.)

9. Follow the same procedure as #7, only this time change just the ending sound or letter card to make new words. (Example: man, map, mat, etc.)

10. Follow the same procedure as #7, only this time change just the short vowel sound or letter card to make new

words. (Example: pan, pen, pin, etc.)

11. Say a short vowel word and see if your child can use the sound or letter cards to make the word. Whenever time permits, have your child extend this activity by recording the word on a piece of paper.

12. Word dictation—give your child a pencil and paper. Say a simple word he/she has previously worked on and have your child write it down. Praise your child for his/her efforts and check the word/words frequently as you do this activity.

Long Vowels

1. Talk to your child about how long vowels "say their own name," or sound like the name of the letter. Also, help him/her to understand that when a vowel "says its own name," it usually needs another vowel with it—for example, "cake," "boat," "teeth."

2. Parents, you can use most of the activities listed for short vowel words for long vowel words with a few minor changes.

0 +0	1 +0	2 +0	3 +0
7	8	9	10
4 +0	5 +0	6 +0	7 +0
3	4	5	6
8 +0	9 +0	10 +0	1 +1
9	0	1	2

10 − 0 3	10 − 1 2	10 − 2 1	10 − 3 0
10 − 4 7	10 − 5 6	10 − 6 5	10 − 7 4
10 − 8 2	10 − 9 10	10 −10 9	9 − 0 8

2 + 1	2 + 2	3 + 1	3 + 2
5	6	7	8
3 + 3	4 + 1	4 + 2	4 + 3
1	2	3	4
4 + 4	5 + 1	5 + 2	5 + 3
6	7	8	0

9 − 1 5	9 − 2 4	9 − 3 4	9 − 4 3
9 − 5 7	9 − 6 6	9 − 7 5	9 − 8 6
9 − 9 8	8 − 0 7	8 − 1 6	8 − 2 8

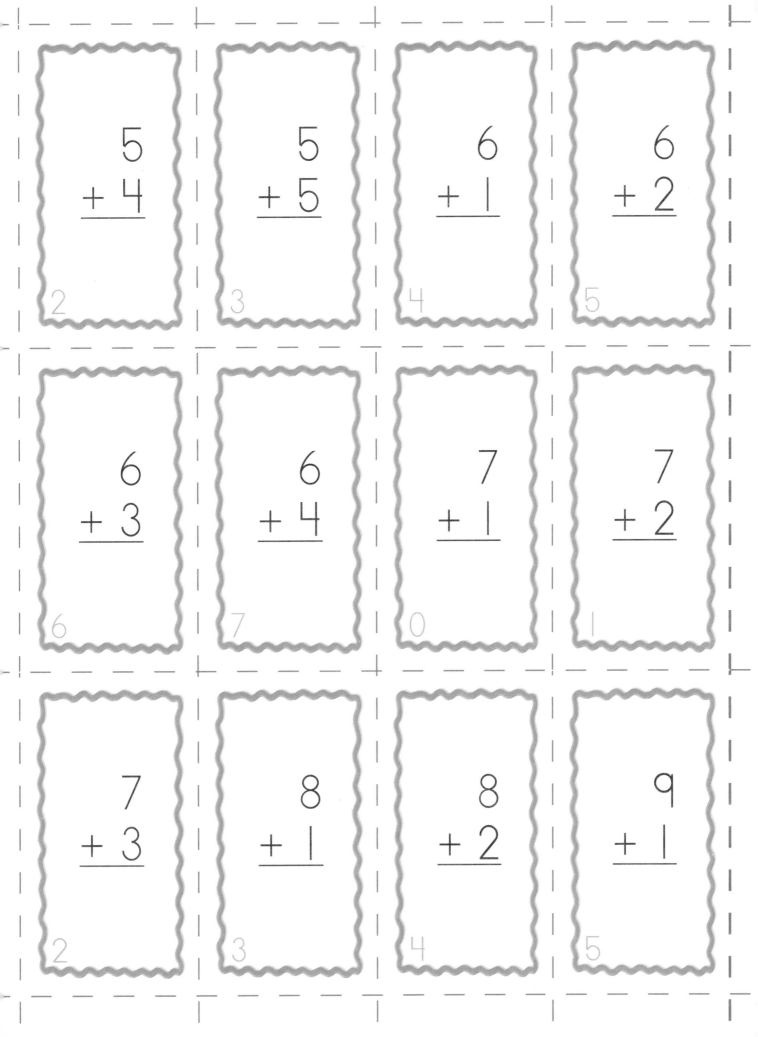

$$\begin{array}{r} 5 \\ + 4 \\ \hline \end{array}$$

2

$$\begin{array}{r} 5 \\ + 5 \\ \hline \end{array}$$

3

$$\begin{array}{r} 6 \\ + 1 \\ \hline \end{array}$$

4

$$\begin{array}{r} 6 \\ + 2 \\ \hline \end{array}$$

5

$$\begin{array}{r} 6 \\ + 3 \\ \hline \end{array}$$

6

$$\begin{array}{r} 6 \\ + 4 \\ \hline \end{array}$$

7

$$\begin{array}{r} 7 \\ + 1 \\ \hline \end{array}$$

0

$$\begin{array}{r} 7 \\ + 2 \\ \hline \end{array}$$

1

$$\begin{array}{r} 7 \\ + 3 \\ \hline \end{array}$$

2

$$\begin{array}{r} 8 \\ + 1 \\ \hline \end{array}$$

3

$$\begin{array}{r} 8 \\ + 2 \\ \hline \end{array}$$

4

$$\begin{array}{r} 9 \\ + 1 \\ \hline \end{array}$$

5

8	8	8	8
− 3	− 4	− 5	− 6
8	7	10	9

8	8	7	7
− 7	− 8	− 0	− 1
9	8	10	9

7	7	7	7
− 2	− 3	− 4	− 5
10	10	9	10

7 − 6	7 − 7	6 − 0	6 − 1
4	0	1	2
6 − 2	6 − 3	6 − 4	6 − 5
0	1	2	3
6 − 6	5 − 0	5 − 1	5 − 2
0	1	2	3

5 − 3 ___ 5	5 − 4 ___ 6	5 − 5 ___ 0	4 − 0 ___ 1
4 − 1 ___ 1	4 − 2 ___ 2	4 − 3 ___ 3	4 − 4 ___ 4
3 − 0 ___ 3	3 − 1 ___ 4	3 − 2 ___ 5	3 − 3 ___ 0

ō ū ă ĕ

ĭ ŏ ŭ

$$\begin{array}{r} 2 \\ -\ 0 \\ \hline \end{array}$$

$$\begin{array}{r} 2 \\ -\ 1 \\ \hline \end{array}$$

$$\begin{array}{r} 2 \\ -\ 2 \\ \hline \end{array}$$

$$\begin{array}{r} 1 \\ -\ 0 \\ \hline \end{array}$$

$$\begin{array}{r} 1 \\ -\ 1 \\ \hline \end{array}$$

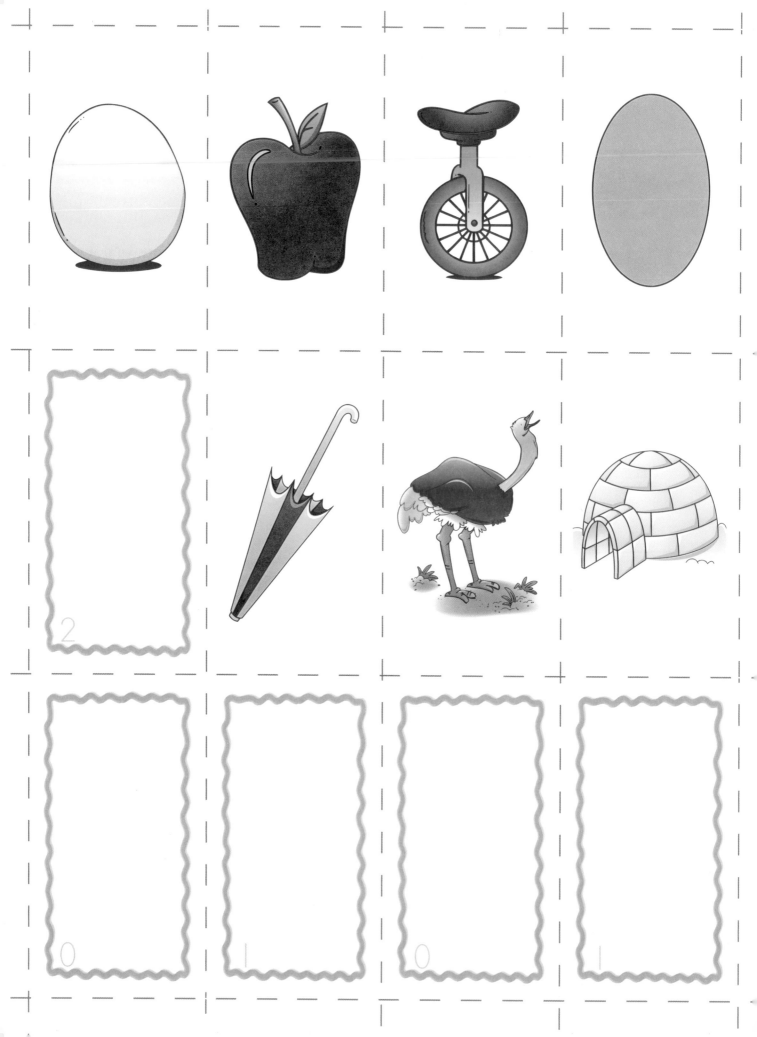

Congratulations!

_____
your name

HAS COMPLETED

Summer Bridge Activities™

AND IS READY FOR THE 2ND GRADE!

Ms. Hansen   *Mr. Fredrickson*

Ms. Hansen   Mr. Fredrickson   Parent's Signature

WWW.SUMMER BRIDGE ACTIVITIES.COM